Camp Cookbook

FEATURING CAMP RECIPES FOR FIXING BOTH AT HOME AND IN THE FIELD

With Field Stories by Dale A. Burk

Camp Cookbook

FEATURING CAMP RECIPES FOR FIXING BOTH AT HOME AND IN THE FIELD

With Field Stories by Dale A. Burk

Copyright 1993 By Dale A. Burk

ISBN 0-912299-52-5

STONEYDALE PRESS PUBLISHING COMPANY
205 Main Street • Drawer B
Stevensville, Montana 59870
Phone: 406-777-2729

TABLE OF CONTENTS

Cover Photograph: *A tent camp in Oregon provides the setting of this scene in which Helen "Rusty" Beckel of Portland is shown preparing a meal. Our thanks to Rusty and husband, Bob, of Beckel Canvas Co., for making arrangements to allow us to take pictures at their camp. (Photo by Dale A. Burk)*

Editor's Note: This recipe, in her own handwriting, is for Lena Jane Bacon's "Soft Molasses Cookies." The typeset recipe is on Page 92.

Dec 1970

Makes about 5 do

Here's what's cookin Soft Molasses Cookies Serves

Recipe from the kitchen of Gram Bacon

⅓ cup shortening

¾ cup brown sugar

¾ cup molasses

2 eggs (beaten)

¾ cup butter milk or other sour milk

2 teaspoons soda dissolved in buttermilk, 1 teaspoon salt 1½ teaspoons ginger 1 teaspoon nutmeg Add salt & spices to 2 cups flour stir into above mixture. Then add enough flour to make soft dough. chill and roll to about ⅛ inch thickness, cut with cookie cutters, Bake on greased baking sheet 12 to 15 minutes at 350 Temperature.

Good with just sugar sprinkled on dough when rolled out or with plain powdered sugar frosting this is my favorite christmas cookie

DEDICATION

This book is fondly dedicated to the memory of my paternal grandmother, Lena Jane Bacon, who worked as a camp cook for almost forty years all the way from remote settings at the famous backcountry lodges in Glacier National Park on to camps in the Bob Marshall Wilderness, and at numerous dude or guest ranches and logging camps across Montana. Many was the time that packers and others who'd heard she was at a specific camp would travel miles out of their way to "stop by" and enjoy one of her meals and a couple or more slices of her famous apple or pumpkin pie.

She believed in simplicity, hard work, a bedrock faith in God, her family, good literature, and the notion that for people to work hard they must be fed healthful, nourishing, and tasteful fare, with proportions ample to their need and nourishing to the spirit as well. She had no need for the measuring devices we outline for recipes in this book, road maps essential for most of us mere mortal cooks to get the proper mixings for one kind of fare or another. For her it was a handful of this and a pinch or two of that added by busy, work-worn hands and a caring spirit. She cooked and cared for others as well as her large family, and her grandchildren and great-grandchildren, from the days of her youth into her late eighties and no one, ever, left her table whatever the setting — backcountry camp, fancy guest ranch, or her home — without realizing that they had just experienced a lovingly-prepared meal of extraordinary dimensions.

INTRODUCTION

There is, or should be at least, a rationale behind every cookbook, a purpose for its existence, a focus of intent or need that it fills. That is the case with *Camp Cookbook*. In talking with hundreds of outdoor people around the country who face varying needs of what to fix and how to fix it to simplify cooking in the hunting or fishing camp, it became obvious that a direct and sharply-focused, simplified, cookbook was needed.

The focus of this cookbook is simple: to provide fundamental, practical recipes for preparing nourishing, healthful meals for outdoors-oriented people in two basic settings, the outdoor camp itself and at home for the ultimate purpose of taking afield with you (though no one will begrudge you should you want to fix and eat the meals at home).

We've pulled together in *Camp Cookbook* some basic, long-proven recipes that have proven their worth over decades of use. That's practical and that was the basic philosophy behind the book: if it doesn't work, and hasn't been proven, don't include it. If it does and it meets a camper's needs, whether he or she must fix it at home so it can be taken to camp with them or allow preparation under the more primitive, if varied, settings of the camp, then offer it. The choice, ultimately, of what recipe to use and how and where to fix it is up to the individual cook. Our point was to offer you the choice, but to temper that offer with a sense of practicality, a notion of common sense throughout the entire text. This is, after all, a camp cookbook and not an attempt to pretend that you are bringing an ultra-modern home or fancy kitchen to a wilderness setting. That's a phony notion to begin with and we want no part of that kind of pretentiousness.

At the same time, you'll find a few recipes in *Camp Cookbook* that reach out a bit, that add a bit of zest and history and, well, flavor from various parts of the country and diverse cultural backgrounds. But always, always, you'll find recipes that have both been tried and proven under field, i.e., camp conditions. Consider, for example, the Cajun breakfast treat offered by Roger Morton's "Smothered Potatoes" out of the Oachita River country of southern Arkansas or the famous "Butte Pasties" from the Cornish miners of Montana's early day mining camp at Butte, the "Richest Hill on Earth." Incidentally, one of our recipes for the Butte Pasty comes from Doris Reilly Glass, a direct descendant of those early-day Cornish miners whose delightful carry-with-you stew encased in bread dough became a mainstay of cultural melting pot that was Butte Hill — and richer in table fare, indeed, are we because of that history.

You'll also find a selected number of proven, down-to-earth recipes for wild game and a special grouping of recipes for utilizing buffalo or bison meat, at one time a staple on the western frontier and contemporarily becoming a plentiful and popular, if tasty and nutritious, table fare. For the latter, we are grateful to the American Bison Society for graciously providing a number of recipes utilizing American buffalo.

For some of our other recipes using wild game, we turned to time-tested favorites from sources who were glad to pass along, anonymously, their favorite methods of preparing venison or pheasant or duck, or the salmon or trout, etc. One special recipe source, however, to which you might want to turn are those listings offered from Duncan and Pat Gilchrist of Hamilton, Montana, whose table fare almost exclusively comes from the game and fish they take from the outdoors. For years they lived in Alaska and their recipes demonstrate the simplicity of back country origin: they are easy to fix and delightful to the taste and, if you have any doubt, we turn you either to Duncan's recipe for cooking big game in teriyaki sauce or Pat's recipe for Hamburgers and Tomato Sauce. Each is a treat in and of itself, but then so are dozens of other recipes in the various categories we've offered in *Camp Cookbook*. Give them a try...

APPETIZERS

LOW CALORIE CHICKEN SNACKS

2 1/2 cups ground cooked chicken
1/2 cup grated carrots
1/2 cup minced parsley
1/2 cup chopped onion
3 1/4 cups low-fat mayonnaise
1 1/2 cups ground dry roasted peanuts
1/4 cup margarine, melted

Mix together chicken, parsley, carrots and onion. Add mayonnaise and mix well. Roll into 1 inch balls. Roll balls in ground peanuts. Dip one side of ball in margarine and place on ungreased cookie sheet, margarine side up. Bake at 400 degrees for 15 minutes. Cool 5 minutes before serving. 95 calories, 8 mg sodium per piece.

ONION STICKS

Mix 1 package onion soup mix with 2 sticks (1 cup) butter or margarine.

Trim crusts from 12 slices bread. Spread onion and butter on bread slices; cut into strips. Place strips on ungreased baking sheet. Bake at 375 degrees for 10 minutes.

CHICKEN SPREAD

1 can chicken spread
2 teaspoons mayonnaise or salad dressing
1/2 cup chopped almonds
2 tablespoons sweet pickle relish

Mix together, serve on crackers.

DEVILED EGGS

6 hard boiled eggs, shelled
1/4 cup mayonnaise
1/4 teaspoon salt
Dash of pepper
1 teaspoon mustard
1 teaspoon minced onion
Paprika
Dash of tabasco sauce

Cut eggs in half. Remove yolks and mash. Blend in mayonnaise, salt, pepper, mustard and onion. Fill hollows of whites and sprinkle with paprika.

SAUSAGE WRAP

Cooked sausage links
Crescent dough

Cut sausage links into desired size. Wrap in refrigerated crescent dough. Bake at 400 degrees for 5 minutes or until brown.

SALMON SPREAD

2 cups canned salmon, drained
1 - 8 ounce package cream cheese
1/4 teaspoon liquid smoke
2 tablespoons lemon juice
2 tablespoons grated onion
2 1/2 cups ground nuts (pecans, walnuts, peanuts)

Mix well first five ingredients. Chill and form into a ball and then roll in ground nuts. Serve with crackers.

MEATBALLS AND HOT DOGS

3 pounds ground meat
1 package onion soup mix
1 4 1/2 ounce can deviled ham (optional)
1 egg
1/4 cup bread crumbs
1 pound hot dogs, cut in small pieces
2 14 ounce bottles catsup (or chili sauce)
1 jar apple or grape jelly

Combine ground meat, onion soup mix, deviled ham, egg and bread crumbs. Form into small meatballs. Arrange on cookie sheet and broil until brown on all sides (or brown in skillet).

In skillet over medium-low heat, stir together catsup and jelly until blended. Add meatballs and hot dogs, simmer about 25 minutes.

PORK-FILLED WONTONS

1 package ground pork sausage
1 can water chestnuts, chopped
2 green onions, chopped
30 wonton skins
Oil for frying

Cook sausage, drain. Combine sausage, water chestnuts and onion. Place 1 tablespoon mixture on center of wonton skin. Moisten corners of wonton skin with water and fold like envelope; pinch to seal. Deep fat fry until golden brown. Serve with sweet and sour sauce and Chinese hot mustard.

DEVILED HAM BISCUITS

1 package refrigerator biscuits
1/4 cup butter or margarine
1 4 1/2 ounce can deviled ham
1/4 cup grated parmesan cheese

Cut biscuits in quarters and arrange in two 8-inch round baking dishes. Heat butter and deviled ham until blended. Pour mixture over biscuits, coating them all. Sprinkle with cheese. Bake in 400 degree oven for 15 minutes. Serve hot.

FISH TIDBIT

Here is a simple way to prepare tidbit that makes a perfect unique appetizer for valued friends. Slice a salmon or large trout as thin as possible. If it is semi-frozen so much the better. Soak for several hours in a mixture of lemon juice and cracked coriander. The result is delicious on crackers.

Courtesy Duncan Gilchrist, Hamilton, Montana

RELISH

2 medium heads cabbage or cauliflower
8 medium carrots
8 green peppers — can also use red
12 medium onions

Grind together and add 1/2 cup salt. Let stand 2 hours. Squeeze out brine and add 6 cups sugar, 5 cups vinegar, 1 teaspoon mustard seed and 1 teaspoon celery seed. Do not cook and need not be sealed. Keeps well.

DEVILED EGGS

12 eggs

Boil eggs, remove shells and then slice eggs in half. Remove and mash yolks. Then combine the following with the yolks:

3 tablespoons mayonnaise
1 tablespoon durkee sauce
2 tablespoons sweet pickle relish
1/4 teaspoon garlic powder
1/2 teaspoon seasoned salt
1/4 teaspoon dry mustard
1/4 cup chopped celery
1 tablespoon chopped green onions
1/4 teaspoon pepper
1 teaspoon Worcestershire sauce

Mix thoroughly and use to fill the white portions of the eggs. Good by itself but you also can sprinkle with paprika and garnish with slices of green olives.

NACHOS

1 package tortilla chips
1 can refried beans
1 can chopped green chilies or 1 jar Jalapeno strips
2 1/2 cups shredded cheddar or monterey jack cheese

Spread tortilla chips on cookie sheet. Top with beans and green chilies or jalapeno strips. Sprinkle with cheese. Place under broiler for 2 or 3 minutes until cheese melts. Or microwave on high for 2 or 3 minutes until cheese melts.

EVEN A BIBLIOPHILE HAS TO EAT

Long before I even wanted to learn such erudite words as bibliophile, I learned over a middle-of-the-night meal in a wilderness hunting camp that I was one of those kind of people and didn't even know it until that night — though I'd realized from my youthful days in the northwestern Montana town of Kalispell, where I'd spent hundreds of hours reading books at the two libraries in town, the more formal Carnegie City Library and the Flathead County Free Library that put the welcome mat out to working people's kids like me, that I liked books.

In the years that I was growing up just outside Kalispell's city limits, I haunted the town's two libraries, reading a couple of hundred books a year and, always, finding an extra "suggested" book at the counter for me when I left the library. The head librarians at both places always had a book or two there they wanted me to read and it was only later, much later, in life that I realized the profound influence they'd had on both my reading habits and my writing as well as my interest in philosophy, which ultimately was my college major.

But to learn that you were a bibliophile! A phile of anything! But, a LOVER of books! And to come to that realization in a wilderness hunting camp. Why it was almost more than the son of a logger and, at that time, a wilderness hunting guide and packer and would-be writer, could accept, though, on reflection, I've come to realize that the accusation was true. I proved it, beyond question, one horrible, stormy, cold night at a place known as the Spotted Bear in the South Fork of the Flathead at the northern edge of the Bob Marshall Wilderness.

The saga began, however, further upriver along the edge of Silvertip Mountain deep in the wilderness. Cliff Levang, the packer for the hunting camp I was working in, and I had been sent on a mission to bring out a party of hunters in one of our spike camps and the two bull elk they'd taken — with firm orders to get them out before nightfall when a severe pre-winter storm was predicted to hit the area.

As is too often the case in the South Fork, and many other mountainous areas, in late October, predictions on the timing of a storm's arrival are only guesses. Cliff had picked up the announcement of this particular storm over either radio station KGEZ, which we listened to at night for the news and weather forecast, or KOFI, which we caught in the morning over breakfast for the weather and the musings of "Sleepy" George Ostrom, and, incidentally, both of these Kalispell stations are still broadcasting today. The decision subsequently was made to pack out our spike camp on Silvertip a day early and within the hour Cliff and I, with our string of packhorses, had headed up the trail on Harrison Creek on our way to the camp. But we had no chance to beat the storm; the first phase of the storm, gigantic, sloppy-wet snowflakes, hit us just as we rode into the camp and informed our hunters they would have to leave a day early.

We also learned that they'd taken another elk that morning; we'd have to go get it, too, and I got that job while Cliff handled tearing down the spike camp and getting all the hunters' gear in manties. He had them ready to go an hour and a half later when the successful elk hunter and I returned to the campsite with the elk and, after a last warming cup of coffee and a sandwich, we headed down the trail toward the trailhead at Spotted Bear.

Three to four inches of wet snow had already accumulated on the deeply-cut horse trail, which by now had become a continuous stream of accumulated dust and slop, and as darkness overtook us we realized it was going to be a long, wet, cold, and miserable night even if everything went well — which it never does when you're taking a string of loaded horses through the wilderness at night, in a storm. Nothing monumental occurred, however, in spite of one near-wreck along an easy-part of the trail under Spotted Bear Ridge when seven or eight mountain goats appeared out of the mist and heavily-falling snow and dashed from the river-side of the trail right through the middle of our string. A brief bucking frenzy broke out, but the horses were as weary and numbed by the cold as we were and it didn't take long to get things straightened out — though by now, with the storm worsening and the darkness becoming even more profound, the decision was made to send the four hunters on their way while Cliff and I stayed with the slower-moving pack string. In doing so, it actually made things easier for us; we could focus on the demands of handling the string alone and not have the inexperienced hunters either interfering with the string or doing something unexpected and spooking them.

Even so, we didn't get to the corrals at Spotted Bear with our string until two in the morning and by the time we'd taken care of our stock it was almost four. Now there was, nearby, another outfitter's camp along the Spotted Bear River, and in circumstances like this when we were caught by a storm we knew we could find both food and a bunk there. So Cliff and I went to their lodge, expecting to catch a bit of sleep and then eat with the crew and their hunters in the morning.

Not so, however. We walked into the lodge to the smell of freshly-baked bread and the aroma of a rich dinner set before us: mashed potatoes, steaming brown gravy, steaks, and even apple pie. The camp cook, knowing we'd worked all day and traveled throughout the evening and into the night in that blizzard, had not only kept dinner for us — as was the custom in such circumstances in the back country camps — but had, herself, stayed up through the night to prepare for us a special meal which, to this day, I remember as one of the most outstanding of my life.

The final part of that story was fulfilled, however, over the apple pie and a dozenth cup of coffee. Against the far wall was nailed a peach box that served as a book rack and I soon found myself, because then as now it is an almost uncontrollable habit for me to read while I eat, thumbing through the books in that rickety old crate.

My hunger abated, warmth once again having returned to my flesh, I looked through the books figuring I'd read a bit while I finished my pie, and then go to bed. One tattered, thick, maroon book cover caught my eye: Pitamakan, by James Willard Schultz. I couldn't believe it! Schultz, one of my favorite authors, a man who had come West in the latter part of the 19th Century and lived with the Blackfeet for a time, indeed who had married into the tribe, a person whose writing I admired, one for whom I'd set a goal to collect all his books with a commitment to do so without having to pursue the rich collector's route and pay top dollar but simply get them where I could and when I could, simply because I didn't have the money to do otherwise. And here, right before me in the midst of a wilderness hunting camp, was one of his most acclaimed titles, the story of the woman warrior Pitamakan. It didn't matter that the pages were yellowed with age and the corners on many had been torn off. I went to the cook and offered to buy the tattered old book.

But no, it wasn't for sale. It was just one she'd brought to camp with her so the hunters would have something to read. I could simply have it, if I wanted it, she said. It probably would be thrown away at the end of the season anyway. It was, she explained, a book she'd picked up from among those someone else had thrown away at one of the schools where she'd taught in bygone years. "You can have it," she said. "No one else has ever even mentioned an interest in it and, besides, you sound to me like a true bibliophile." She handed me the book firmly, like a former teacher would, and smiled. "I've been one of those most of my life, too." she said. "Take it. It's yours now. I'm glad that someone who cares about such things has it."

And thus came into my possession, because of a sumptuous, caring dinner in a wilderness hunting camp and a camp cook-teacher-bibliophile, a book I cherish to this day, one graciously given and more gladly received, from the hand and heart of lady whose name I never knew but who, whether she knew it or not, helped lock in for all time a part of my personality. All I know is that I came to her table in that camp, in the middle of the night, cold and tired and wet and hungry, and I left with my body and my mind and spirit nourished. I was then and am now, truly, like her, a bibliophile. And glad of it.

# # # # #

BREADS

DINNER ROLLS

1 medium-sized potato
2 yeast cakes
1 cup sugar
2 teaspoons salt
Flour to make stiff dough
2 tablespoons butter

Boil and mash potato. Add to water in which it was boiled and make three cups of mash. Then dissolve the yeast cakes in lukewarm water. Add 1 cup of sugar, 2 teaspoons salt, flour to make stiff dough and 2 tablespoons butter. Cool the mixture of potato, water and sugar, add yeast and let stand for 15 to 20 minutes (until it bubbles). Then add salt and flour and, finally, butter. Let rise until it doubles in size. Knead dough down and let rise again. It is best to cut rolls 20 to 30 minutes before baking. Provides a good supply of dinner rolls.

BUTTERHORNS

1 cake yeast or powdered yeast placed in 1/4 cup lukewarm water
1 cup more lukewarm water
1/2 cup lard or shortening
1 teaspoon salt
1 tablespoon sugar
2 eggs
About 5 cups flour

Mix above ingredients into a dough. Divide dough into 4 parts - let rise until double in bulk. Roll out into round shape and cut into six pie-shaped wedges. Brush with melted butter. Roll up from large end. Shape like horseshoe and let rise until light. Bake in hot oven (450 degrees) until brown.

BANANA BREAD

2 ripe medium bananas, peeled
3/4 cup packed brown sugar
1/2 cup butter or margarine, softened
1 egg
1/4 cup dairy sour cream
1 teaspoon vanilla
2 1/4 cups flour
1 teaspoon baking powder
1/2 teaspoon baking soda
1/2 teaspoon salt
1/2 teaspoon ground cinnamon
1 cup chopped walnuts

If doing at home slice bananas into blender, or you can mash them with a fork (should have 1 cup). Beat sugar and butter until light and fluffy. Beat in egg. Beat in banana, sour cream and vanilla until blended. Combine flour, baking powder, soda, salt and cinnamon. Add to banana mixture. Beat until blended. Stir in walnuts. Pour into 9x5x2-inch loaf pan. Bake in 350 degree oven 65 to 70 minutes until toothpick inserted comes out clean. Cool in pan 10 minutes. Invert on wire rack to completely cool.

SPOON BREAD

4 cups milk
1 1/3 cups yellow cornmeal
4 eggs, well beaten
2 tablespoons melted butter
4 teaspoons baking powder
1 teaspoon salt

Cook 2 cups of milk, salt and cornmeal into mush. Add rest of milk, eggs, baking powder and butter. Stir until smooth. Bake in medium oven 30-40 minutes.

PACKER'S BREAD

*Versions of this recipe are found all over under a variety of names:
packer's bread, logging camp bread, sheepherder's camp bread, line
camp bread, etc. You prepare it in two stages and it can be made at
home or in camp with even the most primitive equipment.*

Starter: Mix 2 cups white flour and 2 tablespoons sugar with enough
warm water to make a medium batter. Pour this in a glass jar or
similar container. Cover with a thin cloth over the top (seal with a
piece of tied string or a rubber band) and set out of the way where
warm. Let stand for 2-4 days, until the batter looks bubbly (that
means it's fermenting) and you hear a hissing noise coming from the
mixture. Once that's occurred, put a large cup of this starter in a pint
jar or similar container and store in a cool spot for use as a starter
on your next makings of sourdough bread or pancakes.

The basic bread mix: Add the following ingredients to the starter
batch you still have.

1/2 teaspoon salt
1/4 cup shortening
2 tablespoons sugar
1 cup warm water
Add 1 1/2 cups flour

Stir thoroughly and add flour to make a stiff dough. Knead well or
until smooth. Then place in a large, well greased pan and let rise
until it has almost doubled in bulk. Shape into loaves and once again
let the dough rise until doubled. Then bake in a hot oven (375
degrees to 400 degrees) for 40 to 50 minutes. You can also roll the
dough to about 1/2 inch and break into smaller units (cutting with an
upturned coffee cup works well) or pat them flat. Put these smaller
units on greased skillet or a small pan, allow to rise until doubled in
size and then bake in a covered skillet or a Dutch oven. Works
wonderfully over a camp fire. You also can bake in a hot oven for
25 to 30 minutes. Often they were baked in a covered skillet or
Dutch oven over an open fire.

DUMPLINGS

1 1/2 cups flour
1/2 teaspoon salt
2 level teaspoons baking powder
1 level tablespoon shortening
1 egg
1/2 to 3/4 cup milk to make stiff dough like biscuits

Mix above ingredients. Knead — break off pieces about the size of a golf ball. Drop in broth enough to cover dumplings well. Have broth boiling. Cover and do not raise cover until cooked — about 20 to 25 minutes.

SPATZLI (SWISS RECIPE) LITTLE DUMPLINGS

1 egg, beaten
1/2 cup flour
1/2 teaspoon salt

Mix. Makes very stiff batter. Put on flat plate and with knife dipped in hot water whittle off in small chunks into a kettle 2/3 full of boiling, salted water. When done or they rise to the top, strain off water. Have ready browned onions and grated cheese. Arrange in bowl a layer of dumplings, layer of cheese, then pour sizzling hot onions and bacon drippings over dumplings.

Courtesy Elga Haff, Hamburg, Germany

APRICOT BREAD

1 can (17 ounces) apricot halves
2 cups sifted all-purpose flour
1 teaspoon baking powder
1/2 teaspoon baking soda
1/2 teaspoon salt
1/2 cup chopped walnuts
2/3 cup sugar
1/3 cup vegetable shortening
2 eggs
3 tablespoons orange juice

Drain apricots, reserving syrup. Puree apricots in electric blender or force through food mill. Add enough apricot syrup to puree to measure 1 cup. Sift together flour, baking powder, soda and salt; mix with nuts. Cream together sugar and shortening in bowl; beat in eggs. Stir in orange juice and apricot puree. Add flour-nut mixture and mix well. Pour batter into greased 9x5x3-inch loaf pan or six greased 4 1/2 x 2 1/2 x 1 1/4 inch pans. Bake in 350 degree oven until bread tests done, about 40 to 45 minutes for large loaf and about 25 to 30 minutes for small loaves. Cool 10 minutes; remove from pan, cool on rack.

LOGGING CAMP TOAST

Slice of bread
Salt

Here's a trick that comes out of the old logging camps: Sprinkle salt on a heated frying pan or griddle and then place the bread over the salt. Watch carefully and turn over to do both sides. The salt prevents the heat from hitting the bread directly and you end up with an excellent piece of toast. Works well with cornbread, muffins or biscuits too.

PUMPKIN NUT BREAD

2 cups sifted flour
2 teaspoons baking powder
1/2 teaspoon soda
1 teaspoon salt
1 teaspoon cinnamon
1/2 teaspoon nutmeg
1 cup canned pumpkin (or fresh, cooked and mashed)
1 cup sugar
1/2 cup milk
2 eggs
1/4 cup softened butter
1 cup chopped pecans

Preheat oven to 350 degrees. Sift together first 6 ingredients. Combine pumpkin, sugar, milk and eggs in mixing bowl. Add dry ingredients and butter; mix until well blended. Stir in nuts. Spread in well-greased 9x5x3-inch loaf pan. Bake at 350 degrees for 45 to 55 minutes or until toothpick inserted in center comes out clean.

BEATEN BISCUITS

2 cups flour
2 teaspoons baking powder
1 tablespoon sugar
1/2 teaspoon salt

Sift or stir together. Then add evaporated milk to make a stiff batter - about 1/2 cup. Prepare the baking pan by placing cooking oil or bacon drippings in it. Pour the extra grease (about 3 tablespoons) into the batter. Beat until smooth and then pour or spoon carefully into the pan. Can be baked in a hot oven until brown or in a Dutch oven or covered frying pan over a campfire.

CORN BREAD

1 cup sifted white flour
3 teaspoons baking powder
1/2 teaspoon salt
1 cup yellow corn meal
1 cup milk
2 eggs, beaten
1/4 cup honey or maple syrup
1/4 cup melted butter or bacon drippings

Combine and sift first 3 ingredients into bowl. Stir in corn meal. Combine milk, eggs, honey or syrup and melted butter or bacon drippings; mix. Add liquids to dry ingredients; stir only until dry ingredients are moistened. Pour into greased 8-inch square baking pan and bake in hot oven (425 degrees) until done and lightly browned, about 20 minutes.

CORN MUFFINS

1 can (8 3/4 ounces) whole kernel corn
1 egg, slightly beaten
1 teaspoon instant minced onion
3 tablespoons crumbled bacon bits
1 package (12 ounces) corn muffin mix
Milk

Preheat oven to 400 degrees. Drain liquid from corn into a measuring cup; add enough milk to make amount called for on corn muffin mix package (each trade product is different). Combine with corn, egg, mustard and onion. Add to muffin mix in medium bowl; stir just until moistened. Spoon batter into greased muffin cups, filling half-full. Bake at 400 degrees for 15 to 18 minutes or until tops are golden. Best served warm. Makes a dozen muffins.

OATMEAL MUFFINS

3 cups quick cooking oatmeal
3 tablespoons sugar
3 teaspoons baking powder
3/4 teaspoon salt
1 1/2 cups milk
1 egg, beaten
3 tablespoons cooking oil or melted shortening

Combine first 4 ingredients in bowl and mix thoroughly. Combine milk, egg and oil or melted shortening; beat slightly. Add liquids to dry ingredients and stir until dry ingredients are moistened. Fill greased muffin cups about 3/4 full. Bake in hot oven (425 degrees) until done and lightly browned, about 25 minutes. Makes a dozen muffins.

OATMEAL PINEAPPLE BREAD

4 eggs
1 1/2 cups sugar
2 1/2 cups flour
2 teaspoons salt
2 teaspoons soda
1 1/2 cups quick oats
2 1/2 cups crushed pineapple, undrained
3 cups (10 ounces) flaked coconut

Combine eggs and sugar and beat for a couple of minutes until light. Sift flour, salt and soda; then add to egg mixture and blend until smooth. Add remaining ingredients and mix very well. Spoon into two greased and floured 9x5 inch loaf pans. Bake at 325 degrees for one hour. Remove from pan immediately and serve warm or cold.

APPLESAUCE PANCAKES

1 cup sifted flour
1/2 teaspoon salt
1 1/2 teaspoons baking powder
1 cup apple sauce
1/4 teaspoon cinnamon
1 tablespoon sugar
1/4 teaspoon vanilla extract
2 eggs, separated
1 1/2 teaspoons melted butter or margarine

Sift flour, salt and baking powder into mixing bowl. Blend in next 4 ingredients. Beat egg yolks and add with butter. Beat egg whites until stiff and fold in. Pour batter lightly for each pancake onto hot greased griddle. Turn cakes once. Makes 8 to 10 medium-sized pancakes.

APPLE PANCAKES AND SAUSAGE

8 ounce package of sausages
1 cup pancake mix
1/4 teaspoon ground nutmeg
1/4 teaspoon ground cinnamon
1/2 cup milk
1 egg
1/2 cup chopped apple

Brown sausages. In a mixing bowl, combine all ingredients except apple. Mix until batter is smooth. Add apple. Pour into a well-greased 2-inch deep baking pan. Arrange sausages on top. Bake in 450 degree heat for 20 minutes. Serve hot with maple syrup.

BUCKWHEAT PANCAKES

1 cup buckwheat flour
1 teaspoon baking powder
1/4 teaspoon salt
1 egg
1 1/4 cups sour milk* or buttermilk
1/2 teaspoon baking soda
1 tablespoon cooking oil or melted shortening
1 tablespoon molasses

Combine and mix flour, baking powder and salt in bowl; set aside. Combine remaining ingredients in another bowl in order listed. Add flour mixture; beat just until batter is smooth. For each pancake, pour batter lightly onto hot, greased griddle. Bake until top is covered with bubbles and edges look cooked. Turn, brown second side. Batter tends to thicken as it stands; stir well just before using. Serve with butter and syrup. Makes 8 to 9 cakes.

*To make "sour" milk, measure a teaspoon of vinegar into a cup, add milk and let stand for several minutes before using.

BRAN PANCAKES

1/2 cup 100% bran cereal
1/2 cup pancake mix
2/3 cup milk
1 egg
1 tablespoon vegetable oil

In medium bowl, combine bran cereal and pancake mix. Stir in milk, egg and oil. Let stand for six to seven minutes. Use batter lightly for each pancake and cook on lightly greased griddle, browning on both sides. Makes 8 to 10 medium-sized pancakes.

EASY BREAKFAST ROLLS

1 package frozen dinner rolls (raw dough type)
1 package butterscotch pudding mix
1/2 cup brown sugar
1/2 cup melted butter
1/2 cup chopped walnuts (optional)
Cinnamon to taste

Arrange rolls in greased, shallow pan. Sprinkle with pudding mix. Mix brown sugar, butter and cinnamon together and pour over rolls and pudding. Sprinkle with nuts. Cover with plastic wrap and refrigerate or let set where cool overnight. Bake at 350 degrees for 35 minutes. Remove from pan as soon as done.

OATMEAL PANCAKES

1 1/2 cups baking mix
1 cup regular or quick-cooking oats
1 2/3 cups milk
1 egg

Beat all ingredients with wire whisk or hand beater until smooth. Pour by scant 1/4 cupfuls onto hot griddle (grease if necessary). Cook until edges are dry. Turn and cook until golden brown. Makes about eighteen 4-inch pancakes.
No-cholesterol Oatmeal Pancakes: Substitute skim milk for the milk and 2 egg whites or 1/4 cup frozen (thawed) cholesterol-free egg product for the egg.

BRAN MUFFINS

1 1/4 cups all-purpose flour
1 tablespoon baking powder
1/2 teaspoon salt
1/2 cup sugar
1 1/2 cups bran cereal, or raisin bran cereal
1 1/4 cups milk
1 egg
1/3 cup shortening or vegetable oil

Stir together flour, baking powder, salt and sugar. Set aside. Measure cereal and milk into large mixing bowl and stir to combine. Let stand 1 or 2 minutes or until cereal is softened. Add egg and shortening and beat well. Then add flour mixture and stir until combined. Portion batter evenly into 12 greased muffin pan cups. Bake at 400 degrees about 25 minutes or until lightly browned. Makes 12 muffins.

BREAD

1 quart water (hot)
1 tablespoon salt
2 tablespoons sugar, brown or white
1 cake yeast
5 cups white flour

Beat until smooth and let rise. Add 4 tablespoons grease and 4 tablespoons of rye and graham flour. Let rise until light. Bake slow 1 hour, oven hot at beginning. When putting in rye and graham flour, stir to proper thickness as in white bread. Bake in narrow bread tins.

SUGARED BREAKFAST MUFFINS

Combine in a bowl:
1/2 cup flour
3/4 cup whole wheat flour
2 teaspoons baking powder
1/2 teaspoon salt

Combine in another bowl:
1 beaten egg
1/4 cup melted margarine
1/2 cup milk
1/2 cup packed brown sugar

Combine all ingredients and bake at 375 degrees for 25 minutes.

CORN FRITTERS

1/2 cup sifted flour
3/4 teaspoon baking powder
1/4 teaspoon salt
2 teaspoons sugar
1 egg
1/4 cup milk
1 tablespoon cooking oil
1 cup fresh or canned whole kernel corn

Combine dry ingredients and mix well. Combine remaining ingredients and stir into dry ingredients. Drop by tablespoonfuls into hot oil; about 1/8" in bottom of large frying pan. Fry until golden brown, turning once. Serve with butter and jam, jelly or syrup.

MOLASSES MUFFINS

1 cup sugar
1 cup shortening
1 cup molasses (light)
1 cup sour milk*
Cream together, then add:
4 eggs, one at a time
4 cups flour
1 teaspoon ginger
1/2 teaspoon allspice
1 teaspoon cinnamon
1 teaspoon salt
2 teaspoons soda
1/2 cup nuts
1/2 cup raisins

Mix all together very thoroughly. Makes a large batch of muffins, or you can keep the mixings refrigerated and bake as needed. Bake 20 minutes at 350 degrees.

*To make "sour" milk, add 1 teaspoon of vinegar to 1 cup milk and let sit a minute.

GRILLED BREAD

Combine: 2 cups bisquick, 1/3 cup sesame seed, 1/2 teaspoon salt. Stir in 2/3 cup milk. Beat vigorously until stiff. Knead 8-10 times on lightly floured surface. Divide dough in half. Pat each half into a rectangle. Cut in half lengthwise.

Grill strips 5 inches from coals 3-4 minutes on each side. Cut each into 4 pieces. Serve hot with butter.

CASSEROLES
&
MAIN DISHES

BUTTE PASTIES

2 pounds meat (London broil or skirting meat cut in small squares. Any good cut of beef or venison will do.)
5 or 6 medium potatoes
3 medium onions
3 or 4 carrots
1 rutabaga

Make crust — use a little less shortening than for pies.

Filling:
Meat: London Broil or Skirting is a good choice (if available), otherwise any good cut of beef or venison is good. Cut in small squares.
Vegetables: Potatoes — chop fairly small. Onions — chopped (green onions can be used.) Carrots or rutabagas optional — chopped.
Put the filling in a bowl and let set for a short while. (This makes for a more moist and tasty pastie.) Add salt and pepper.

Roll crust same as for a pie — put the filling on half and fold the top over — crimp edges and bake at 375 degrees for 45 to 50 minutes depending on size.

About 10 or 15 minutes before removing from the oven — melt some butter or margarine in hot water and put a teaspoon or two in the holes of the crust on each pastie.

Courtesy Doris Reilly Glass, Clinton, Montana

BUTTE PASTIES

Filling:
1 pound of ground meat
3 large potatoes
3 large carrots
1/2 onion
Salt
Pepper

Dice potatoes, carrots and onions. Mix with ground meat, salt and pepper and set aside.

Crust:
2 1/4 cups flour
1 teaspoon salt
2/3 cup shortening
6-8 tablespoons cold water

Stir together flour and salt. Cut in shortening until size of small peas. Sprinkle 1 tablespoon water over part of mixture. Toss with fork and push to side of bowl. Repeat until all is moist. Roll out handful of dough. Mound filling on one-half. Fold over and pinch closed. Poke two vents with fork. Bake at 350 degrees on ungreased cookie sheet for 35 to 45 minutes.

Courtesy Beth Burk, Lolo, Montana

BEEF STEW

4 to 4 1/2 pounds lean beef chuck
4 tablespoons shortening
2 quarts water
1 tablespoon Worcestershire sauce
1 tablespoon lemon juice
l large grated onion
1 good-sized rutabaga
4 bay leaves
2 cloves minced garlic

2 tablespoons of salt
1 teaspoon of pepper
1 teaspoon of paprika
2 dashes ground cloves
2 teaspoons of sugar or sugar substitute
2 cans small white onions
2 cans potatoes or 4 large potatoes
2 bunches sliced carrots
1 cup flour

Cover the meat in flour and brown on all sides in hot shortening. Add water, Worcestershire sauce, lemon juice, garlic and other seasoning before bringing to a boil in a large Dutch oven or kettle. Simmer for 2 hours, being sure to check if more water is needed. Add carrots and cook for 15 minutes. Then add canned potatoes and onions and cook for another 12 minutes, longer if you use uncanned potatoes.

BEEF STEW

3 tablespoons oil
2 pounds stewing beef or lamb, cut in 2-inch cubes
1 beef bouillon cube
2 teaspoons salt
1 bay leaf
1/4 teaspoon crushed dried thyme leaves
4 1/2 cups water
6 carrots, cut in 3-inch strips
12 small white onions
1/4 cup corn starch

In skillet heat oil over medium heat. Add meat and brown on all sides. Add next 4 ingredients and 4 cups of the water. Cover and bring to boil. Then reduce heat and simmer for 1 1/2 hours. Add carrots and onions. Simmer 1/2 hour or until tender. Mix corn starch and 1/2 cup water. Stir into beef mixture and bring to boil, stirring constantly. Boil for 1 minute. Makes 6 servings.

STEW

2 pounds stew meat
3 carrots, cut in pieces
1 box frozen peas
2 onions, cut in pieces
2 potatoes, cut in pieces
1 can tomato soup
1/2 can water
1 teaspoon salt
Pepper
1 bay leaf

Mix all ingredients in large casserole or large pot with lid. Do not brown meat first. Bake at 275 degrees for 5 hours. For a little zest to taste, add 1 rutabaga cut in pieces.

IRISH STEW

6 medium potatoes (about 2 pounds) peeled and thinly sliced
2 pounds lean, bone-in lamb or 1 1/2 pounds boneless lamb, cut
into 1 1/2-inch pieces
2 medium onions, peeled and sliced
1 teaspoon salt
1/4 teaspoon pepper
1/4 teaspoon thyme
1 teaspoon dried summer savory
2 tablespoons minced fresh parsley, or 1 1/2 teaspoons dried
1 1/2 cups water

In Dutch oven layer half the potatoes, and then all the lamb and
onions. Combine salt, pepper, thyme and summer savory. Sprinkle
half of salt mixture and 1 tablespoon of the parsley over onions.
Layer remaining potatoes and sprinkle with remaining salt mixture.
Pour water over all and bring to boil. Cover, reduce heat and
simmer gently 2 to 2 1/2 hours until lamb is tender. Add water as
needed to maintain level about 1 inch in bottom of pan. Sprinkle
with remaining parsley at serving time. Serves 6.

ANOTHER IRISH STEW

2 pounds lamb or beef, cut into 1 inch cubes
1/4 cup flour
1 teaspoon salt
Ground black pepper
Cooking oil
1 medium onion, sliced
1 can (16 oz.) mixed vegetables, undrained
1 can (16 oz.) tomatoes, undrained
1 can (8 oz.) baking powder biscuits

Coat lamb cubes with a mixture of the flour, salt and pepper and brown in cooking oil in a Dutch oven. Stir in sliced onion and cook until clear. Then add vegetables and tomatoes. Cover and bake in a preheated 325 degree oven for 1 1/2 hours. Skim off excess fat and place biscuits over stew. Cook uncovered for about 30 minutes, or until biscuits are browned and meat is tender. Serves 8.

SAUSAGE STEW

1 can (10 1/2 ounces) condensed beef broth
1 cup water
1/8 teaspoon pepper
1 bay leaf
2 medium onions, quartered
6 carrots, pared, cut in julienne pieces
1 1/2 cups diced celery
2 potatoes, pared, diced
2 tablespoons water
1 tablespoon all-purpose flour
1 pound smoked sausage, cut in 1/2 inch pieces
Salt to taste
Grated Parmesan cheese

Combine broth, 1 cup water, pepper, bay leaf, and vegetables except potatoes in a 4-quart saucepot. Cover and simmer for 10 minutes. Add potatoes and cook until vegetables are tender. Remove bay leaf. Mix 2 tablespoons water with flour; stir into vegetables. Add sausage and increase heat until all is hot. Add salt. Top each serving with cheese. 6 to 8 servings.

IRISH STEW CHICKEN

2 medium carrots, cut into 1/4 inch dices
2 medium onions, sliced
2 tablespoons flour
3 cups chicken broth, divided usage
2 medium potatoes, peeled and sliced 1/8 inch thick
1/2 teaspoon salt
1/8 teaspoon pepper
2 medium tomatoes, sliced
1 package (32 ounces) frozen fully-cooked fried chicken
5 slices bacon, cut in half

Place carrots and onions in saucepan and toss with flour. Stir in 2 cups broth and heat to boiling. Boil for 1 minute and then set aside. In 9-inch baking dish, layer potato slices and sprinkle with salt and pepper. Spread the carrot-onion mixture evenly over potatoes and layer with tomato slices. Place the chicken parts on top of tomatoes and top with bacon strips. Pour the remaining 1 cup broth over chicken, being sure to moisten each piece. Heat in 375 degree oven for 45 to 50 minutes until vegetables are tender. Makes 6 servings.

WESTERN STYLE BARBECUE

4 frankfurters cut in 1-inch pieces
2 tablespoons butter or margarine
1 can (19 1/4 ounces) bean with ham soup
1 can (12 ounces) whole kernel corn with sweet peppers, drained
1 can (8 ounces) lima beans, drained
1/2 cup barbecue sauce

Brown frankfurters in butter in a saucepan. Add the remaining ingredients, increase heat slightly while stirring occasionally. Garnish with green pepper rings to serve. Makes about 5 cups.

STROGANOFF

1 pound ground beef
1 can (4 ounces) sliced mushrooms, drained
1/2 cup chopped onion
1 teaspoon salt
2 cups water
1 beef bouillon cube
1 1/2 cups instant rice
1/2 cup sour cream

Brown ground beef quickly with mushrooms, onion and salt in large skillet, stirring frequently. Stir in water and bouillon cube. Bring to a full boil. Stir in rice. Reduce heat; cover and simmer 5 minutes. Remove from heat. Stir in sour cream. Garnish with chopped parsley, if desired. Makes 4 servings.

VENISON STROGANOFF

1 pound cubed venison
1/8 to 1/4 pound butter
Minced garlic
1/2 cup minced onion
1 6-ounce can mushrooms or fresh mushrooms
Sour cream
2 cups water

Flour and brown meat in butter. Then add garlic, onion and brown. Add mushrooms with juice, add water, cover and simmer 30 minutes or until tender. Add sour cream just before serving. Serve over cooked noodles or rice and also very good over mashed potatoes for a real tasty, filling camp dinner.

BEEF STROGANOFF

2 pounds boneless chuck, cut 1/2 inch thick
1/2 teaspoon each salt & pepper
1 stick butter (1/4 pound)
4 sliced green onions, white part only
4 tablespoons flour
1 can condensed beef broth
1 teaspoon prepared mustard
1 6-ounce can sliced mushrooms
1/3 cup dairy sour cream
Steamed rice

Remove fat and gristle from meat and cut meat across the grain in strips 2 inches long. Sprinkle with salt and pepper. Heat skillet, add butter, saute meat quickly and then brown. Push meat to one side. Add onions, cook slowly a few minutes and then push aside. Stir flour into drippings and add beef broth. Bring to a boil, stirring all the while. Turn heat down, stir in mustard, cover pan and let simmer 1 hour or until meat is tender. A few minutes before serving, add mushrooms and dairy sour cream. Warm and salt to taste. Serve with rice.

CHILI AND RICE SKILLET DINNER

2 cans (15 ounces) chili con carne with beans
1 can (14 1/2 ounces) peeled tomatoes, cut-up
1 can (13 3/4 ounces) beef broth
1 medium green pepper, chopped
2 tablespoons chopped green onion
3/4 cup uncooked white long grain enriched rice

In a 12-inch skillet combine chili, tomatoes, beef broth, green pepper and green onion. Heat to boiling, stirring frequently. Stir in rice. Return to a boil. Reduce heat, cover and let simmer for 25 minutes, stirring frequently. Makes 6 servings.

BEEF AND PEPPER RICE SKILLET

1 1/2 pounds round steak, cut into thin strips
1 tablespoon cooking oil
1 cup sliced onion
1 cup instant rice
1 can (10 1/2 ounces) beef broth
Water
2 tablespoons soy sauce, or to taste
2 green peppers, coarsely chopped
1 jar (2 ounces) sliced pimento, drained

Brown beef in oil in 10-inch skillet. Add onion, rice, beef broth, one soup can of water and soy sauce to beef and then stir. Bring to boil, reduce heat, cover and cook over low heat until liquid is absorbed, about 25 to 30 minutes. Stir in green pepper and pimento. Serve hot. Makes 4 to 6 servings.

LUNCH IN SKILLET

1/2 cup chopped onions
1/2 cup sliced celery
1 cup sliced carrots
1/4 cup chopped green pepper
1 pkg. (10 oz.) frozen peas, thawed
1/4 cup butter or margarine
2 cans (15 oz.) spaghetti with meat balls
1/2 cup milk
1/4 cup shredded Cheddar cheese

In a large skillet saute onions, celery, carrots, pepper and thawed green peas in butter. Add spaghetti with meat balls and milk. Cover and let simmer 5 minutes, stirring constantly. Add shredded Cheddar cheese and stir. Serves 4 to 6.

CASSEROLE

7-ounce package macaroni (2 cups uncooked)
1 can condensed cream of mushroom soup
1 cup milk
1 can (7-ounce) tuna, drained and flaked

Prepare macaroni according to package directions. Drain. Mix macaroni, soup, milk and tuna. Pour into 1 1/2 quart casserole. Bake, uncovered, at 350 degrees for 25-30 minutes. Can be prepared with chicken, ham, franks, luncheon meat, or salmon in place of the tuna. 4 servings.

BACON AND EGG CASSEROLE

1/4 cup margarine or butter
1/8 teaspoon onion salt
1/2 teaspoon freeze-dried chives or parsley flakes
1 cup dry cereal, crushed to measure 3/4 cup
2 tablespoons all-purpose flour
1/2 teaspoon dry mustard
3/4 cup milk
2 hard-cooked eggs, sliced
4 slices bacon, fried crisp and crumbled.

Melt 2 tablespoons of the margarine. Stir in salt and chives. Combine with crushed dry cereal (corn flakes or Rice Krispies work nicely) and set aside. Then melt the remaining 2 tablespoons margarine in small saucepan over low heat. Stir in flour and mustard. Add milk gradually, stirring until smooth. Cook until mixture thickens and boils, stirring constantly. Set aside. Then, in two greased 9-ounce custard cups or individual casseroles, layer half the sliced eggs, half the crumbled bacon, half the sauce and half the cereal mixture. Repeat layers. Bake at 350 degrees for 15 to 20 minutes or until thoroughly heated. Makes 2 servings.

CHICKEN CASSEROLE

1 can (8 ounces) chicken noodle soup
1 can (5 ounces) boned chicken
1 can (8 ounces) cream of mushroom soup
1 cup cooked noodles
1/2 cup Colby or Cheddar cheese, grated
1 tablespoon butter
1/3 cup celery, chopped
1/3 cup onion, chopped

Melt butter in saucepan, add celery and onion. Saute a few minutes. Combine all remaining ingredients with sauteed vegetables. Pour into a casserole dish. Bake at 350 degrees for 30 minutes. Just before serving, add 1 tablespoon of cheese to top of casserole. Serve when cheese is melted. Serves 4 to 5.

POTATO CASSEROLE

4-5 medium sized potatoes, sliced
2 tablespoons flour
1 teaspoon salt
Dash of pepper
3/4 pound processed cheese, cubed
3/4 cup milk
1/4 cup green pepper, diced
1/4 cup onion, diced

Heat oven to 350 degrees. Coat potatoes with flour, salt and pepper. Heat milk and add cubed cheese. Stir over low heat until cheese melts. Then add green pepper and onion. Make layers with potatoes and sauce and top with sauce. Cook 60 minutes or until potatoes are done. Makes 4-6 servings.

TUNA CASSEROLE

1/3 cup margarine
3 tablespoons corn starch
1/2 teaspoon salt
1/8 teaspoon pepper
3 cups milk
1 onion, chopped
2 cans (7 ounces each) tuna, drained and flaked
1 package (8 ounces) elbow macaroni, cooked and drained
1 package (10 ounces) frozen peas, thawed
1 cup shredded Cheddar cheese

In saucepan melt margarine over medium heat. Stir in corn starch, salt and pepper until smooth. Remove from heat and gradually stir in milk until smooth. Bring to boil over medium heat, stirring constantly, and boil 1 minute. Then add onion. Place remaining ingredients in greased 1-quart casserole. Stir in corn starch mixture. Bake in 350 degree oven 25 to 30 minutes or until heated. Makes 6 servings.

CASSEROLE SUPPER

4 pork chops
1 can (1 pound) peas
1 can (10 3/4 oz) cream of mushroom soup
1/4 cup chopped onion

Arrange chops in a 2-inch dish or frying pan. Combine peas, 1/4 cup pea liquid, soup and onion; pour over chops. Cover, bake at 350 degrees for 50 minutes. Uncover and bake 10 minutes more. Makes 4 servings.

CHICKEN CASSEROLE

1 can (10 3/4 ounces) cream of chicken soup
1 jar (8 ounces) pasteurized process cheese spread
2 cups chopped, cooked or canned chicken
1 can (4 ounces) chopped green chilies, drained
12 corn tortillas
1 can (10 ounces) mild enchilada sauce
1 - 2 cups shredded lettuce
1/2 cup chopped tomato

Preheat oven to 350 degrees. Combine soup and process cheese spread, mixing until well blended. Add chicken and green chilies. Spread 1/2 cup of chicken mixture over bottom of a 1-quart rectangular baking dish. Layer four of the tortillas, dipping each in enchilada sauce, and one third of the remaining chicken mixture; repeat layers two more times. Cover with foil; bake 20 minutes. Remove foil, continue baking 15 minutes. Top with lettuce and tomato. Makes 6 servings.

CORNED BEEF HASH

1 4-ounce package sliced corned beef or pastrami
3 tablespoons cooking oil
1 package frozen, diced potatoes
Salt and pepper to taste
4 poached eggs (optional)

Cut meat into slices and separate. Heat cooking oil in large skillet over medium heat. Then add potatoes. Cover and cook, stirring occasionally until slightly brown. Then add meat, stir, and continue cooking until thoroughly hot. Salt and pepper to taste. Some people like to add poached eggs as an option. If so, place on top of hash. Serves 4.

HOT DOG MACARONI

7 ounce package macaroni (2 cups uncooked)
1/2 cup onion, chopped
1/4 cup green pepper, chopped
2 tablespoons butter or margarine
2 tablespoons flour
1 1/2 cups milk
1 cup carrots, grated
1/2 cup sour cream
1/2 teaspoon salt
1/4 teaspoon dillweed
10 frankfurters, split lengthwise

Prepare macaroni according to package directions. Drain. Saute onion and green pepper in butter until tender. Add flour and cook, stirring constantly for about 2 minutes. Avoid browning. Stir in milk and cook until smooth and thickened. Remove from heat, add macaroni, carrots, sour cream, salt and dillweed. Arrange frankfurters vertically around a deep 1 1/2-quart casserole, pour macaroni mixture in center. Bake at 350 degrees for 25 to 30 minutes. Makes 6 servings.

CORNED BEEF/CABBAGE PIE

4 cups shredded cabbage
1 medium-size onion, chopped
1 tablespoon vegetable oil
1 medium-size cooked potato
4 ounces corned beef, chopped
3/4 cup shredded Muenster cheese
2 eggs
1 cup low-fat milk
2/3 cup Basic Baking Mix (Recipe on Page 62)
1/4 teaspoon each caraway seeds, salt and pepper

Preheat oven to 400 degrees.

Coat inside of 9-inch pie plate with nonstick cooking spray. Saute cabbage and onion in oil in large nonstick skillet until tender, about 10 minutes. Dice potato and stir into skillet with corned beef. Cool slightly; stir in cheese. Spread evenly over bottom of prepared plate.

Combine eggs, milk, baking mix, caraway seeds, salt and pepper in blender or food processor; whirl until smooth. Pour evenly over mixture in pie plate.

Bake in preheated 400 degree oven 30 to 35 minutes until browned on top and knife inserted in center comes out clean. Cool 5 minutes. Cut into wedges to serve. Serves 6.

KNOCKWURST 'N CABBAGE

4 knockwurst sausage
1 tablespoon vegetable oil
2 quarts shredded cabbage
1 large onion, sliced
1 clove garlic, pressed
1 cup thinly sliced carrots
1 pound small new potatoes, peeled and sliced
3/4 cup dry white wine
3/4 cup water
1 teaspoon chicken stock base
1 teaspoon pickling spice
1/2 teaspoon salt

Make two or three slits in each knockwurst. In a large skillet, brown knockwurst in hot oil. Remove from skillet. Then, in the same skillet, saute cabbage, onion, garlic and carrots until onion is soft. Stir in potatoes, wine, water, chicken stock base, pickling spice and salt. Cover and simmer 10 minutes. Add knockwurst; cover and simmer 10 minutes longer. Makes about 4 servings.

STUFFED CABBAGE ROLLS

8 large cabbage leaves
1 can (10 3/4 ounces) condensed tomato soup
1 pound ground beef
1 cup cooked rice
1/4 cup chopped onion
1 egg, slightly beaten
1 teaspoon salt
1/4 teaspoon pepper

Cook cabbage in salted water a few minutes to soften and then drain. Mix 2 tablespoons soup with remaining ingredients. Divide meat mixture among cabbage leaves. Then fold in sides and roll up, using toothpicks to keep together. Place rolls seam side down in a skillet and pour remaining soup over them. Cover and cook over low heat for 40 to 50 minutes, stirring occasionally and spooning sauce over rolls. 4 servings.

CABBAGE ROLLS

1 1/2 pounds ground beef chuck or round
3/4 cup finely chopped onion
1/2 cup oatmeal
1 egg
1 1/4 teaspoons salt
1/2 teaspoon dry mustard
1/4 teaspoon pepper
2 cans (8 ounce each) tomato sauce
8 large cabbage leaves
3 tablespoons white flour with wheat germ
2 tablespoons (packed) brown sugar
1 1/2 teaspoons lemon juice
1 can (8 ounce) tomatoes

Combine first 7 ingredients and 1 can tomato sauce. Mix thoroughly. Divide into 8 equal portions. Cut out the stiff back ridge from each cabbage leaf. Dip 2 cabbage leaves at a time into boiling water. Cook until cabbage is limp; drain and chill in cold water. Drain 1 cabbage leaf at a time; dry and place a portion of meat mixture to one end of leaf. Roll up, folding the sides in over meat mixture. Fasten securely with toothpicks or small skewers. Repeat 7 times. Arrange rolls in shallow baking dish. Combine remaining 1 can of tomato sauce, flour, sugar and lemon juice and mix until smooth. Add tomatoes and then stir with spoon or ladle to break up tomatoes. Pour over cabbage rolls. Cover dish with aluminum foil, crimping it securely to edge of dish. Bake in 350 degrees for 75 to 80 minutes. Uncover, spoon sauce over rolls. Bake uncovered about 10 to 12 minutes until sauce thickens and meat is tender. Baste with sauce a few times during baking.

MACARONI AND CHEESE PIZZA

1 package macaroni and cheese
2 eggs
1 8-ounce can tomato sauce
1 4-ounce can mushrooms
1/4 cup chopped onions
1 cup chopped green pepper
1 teaspoon oregano
1 teaspoon basil
1 cup pepperoni slices (or whatever you want)
1 cup mozzarella cheese, grated
1 cup cheddar cheese, grated

Prepare macaroni and cheese as directed on package, then add well beaten eggs and mix well. Spread on greased pan and bake at 375 degrees for 10 minutes. Combine tomato sauce and mushrooms, onion, green pepper and seasonings. Spoon over macaroni. Top with meat and cheeses. Continue baking 10 minutes.

POLISH SAUSAGE SKILLET

1 pound smoked Polish sausage, cut in 1/4-inch slices
1/4 cup sliced green onions
2/3 cup sliced celery
1 (4-ounce) can mushroom stems and pieces
1 1/2 cups boiling water
1/4 teaspoon salt
1/4 teaspoon pepper
2 envelopes individual tomato soup mix
1 tablespoon Worcestershire sauce
1 1/2 cups instant rice

Combine smoked polish sausage, onion and celery in large skillet and cook over low heat until vegetables are tender-crisp. Then add mushrooms, water, salt, pepper, soup mix and Worcestershire sauce. Heat until bubbling and then add rice, stir and cover. Turn off heat and allow to stand for 15 minutes. Serves 4 to 6.

BAKED BEANS WITH WIENERS

1 package (16 ounces) bacon
3 cans (1 pound each) baked beans in molasses sauce
1/2 cup chopped onion
1/4 cup firmly packed brown sugar
1 tablespoon molasses
2 teaspoons Worcestershire sauce
1/2 teaspoon dry mustard
1 package (1 pound) wieners

Cut bacon into one-inch pieces and cook in skillet until crisp. Add onion to bacon and cook until tender. Stir in remaining ingredients except wieners. Place wieners on top of beans and heat for about 15 minutes. Makes 4 servings.

CHILI SKILLET SUPPER

8 ounces (about 2 cups) short cut elbow macaroni, uncooked
1 clove garlic, minced
1/4 cup chopped green pepper
1/2 cup chopped onion
1 pound ground beef
1 (18 ounce) can tomatoes, cut up
1 (21 ounce) jar Italian cooking sauce
2 teaspoons salt
2 teaspoons chili powder
1/8 teaspoon pepper

In a large saucepan add garlic, green pepper, onion and ground beef. Brown lightly. Drain off fat. Add tomatoes, Italian cooking sauce and seasonings, mixing well. Bring to boiling and then gradually stir in macaroni. Reduce heat and simmer, stirring occasionally, about 20-25 minutes or until macaroni reaches desired tenderness. Makes about 4 servings.

APPLE SAUSAGE SKILLET

1 pkg. (10 oz.) brown and serve sausage, chunked
1 medium apple, cored and chunked
2 tablespoons butter or margarine
1/4 cup brown sugar
1 can (15 oz.) kidney beans, drained

Brown sausage and apple in butter until apple is tender. Stir in remaining ingredients and heat until steamy hot. Makes 3 to 4 servings.

CHILI

1 pound ground beef
1/2 cup chopped onion
1/2 cup chopped celery
1 can (46 ounces) tomato juice
1 can (1 pound) stewed tomatoes
1 can Mexican style chili beans
1/3 cup uncooked macaroni
1 teaspoon chili powder

In large saucepan, brown first 3 ingredients and drain excess fat. Then stir in remaining ingredients and simmer 30 minutes, stirring occasionally. An excellent and easy-to-make camp dinner. Makes 6 servings.

NACHOS DINNER

1 pound lean ground beef
1 large onion, chopped
1 teaspoon seasoned salt
1/2 teaspoon ground cumin
2 cans (1 pound each) refried beans
1 package (1 1/4 ounce) taco seasoning mix
2 cups grated Monterey Jack cheese
1 can (4 ounces) chopped green chilies
1 cup grated Cheddar cheese
3/4 cup chunky taco sauce
Fried tortilla chips

Garnish with any or all of the following:
1 cup guacamole
1/2 cup dairy sour cream
1/4 cup chopped green onions
1 cup sliced ripe olives

Brown meat and onions. Drain well and season with seasoned salt and cumin. Combine beans and taco seasoning mix and blend thoroughly. Add grated Monterey Jack cheese and mix together. Spread beans in a shallow, oval (10 x 15 inch) baking dish. Cover with browned meat and onions. Sprinkle chilies over meat; top with Cheddar cheese. Pour chunky taco sauce over cheese. Bake uncovered in a 400 degree oven about 25 minutes or until thoroughly heated. Tuck tortilla chips around edge of platter and garnish as desired. Serves 4 to 6.

SOUTHWEST-STYLE CHILI

1/2 pound chorizo (A Spanish pork sausage)
1/2 pound ground beef
1 1/2 cups chopped onion
2 cloves garlic, minced
1 (15 ounce) can tomato sauce with tomato bits
1 (15 1/2 ounce) can small red beans, undrained
1 (8 ounce) can refried beans
3 to 4 tablespoons chili powder
1 teaspoon ground cumin
1 teaspoon oregano
1/2 teaspoon salt

In good-sized saucepan, cook chorizo, beef, 1 cup onion and garlic until onion is soft. Spoon off excess fat. Add tomato sauce, red beans, refried beans and seasonings and mix thoroughly. Cover and let simmer 10 to 15 minutes, stirring a couple of times. For added zest, cover each serving with uncooked, chopped onion. Makes 4 servings.

EXTRA-HOT SOUTHWEST CHILI

2 pounds chili meat (coarsely ground round steak or well-trimmed chuck steak)
1/2 cup cooking oil
1 1/2 cups water (or beer)
1 (8-ounce) can tomato sauce
2 small onions, chopped
1 medium green pepper, finely chopped
5-6 cloves garlic, minced
1 teaspoon oregano
1 teaspoon ground cumin
4 tablespoons chili powder
1 teaspoon granulated sugar
Cayenne pepper
4-5 medium jalapeno peppers, chopped

In large skillet, braise meat in 1/4 cup oil until brown. Transfer meat to large kettle or pot, leaving liquid in skillet. Add water and tomato sauce to meat, cook over low heat. Saute onion, green pepper and garlic in remaining 1/4 cup oil and liquid in skillet. Add remaining dry ingredients and chopped jalapeno peppers with seeds removed. Simmer about 30 minutes then transfer to pot. Simmer about 2 hours. Ladle off grease that settles on top. Note: Add the cayenne and jalapeno peppers cautiously to taste. Experience will tell you what's best to your taste. Serves 6-8.

HASHED BROWN BARBECUED BEEF

1 cup finely chopped onions
2 pounds boiled potatoes, cold, peeled and cut in very small pieces
2 bay leaves
1/2 cup corn oil
1 #2 can barbecue beef

In saucepan, heat oil. Then slowly cook chopped onions. Stir in the potatoes and the barbecue beef. Season to taste, add the two bay leaves, place mixture in well buttered baking pan, cover with aluminum foil and bake in preheated oven at 350 degrees for 30 minutes. Serve hot with barbecue sauce. Serves 8

BISON STEW

2 pounds cubed bison meat
3 medium potatoes, peeled
6 carrots, peeled and sliced
1 8-ounce can peeled tomatoes
2 6-ounce cans tomato sauce
2 tablespoons cooking oil
2 onions, chopped
1/2 teaspoon pepper
2 teaspoons salt
1/2 cup water

Brown meat in small amount of oil in a large kettle or Dutch oven, then add onion and cook until golden. Add tomato sauce, carrots, peeled tomatoes, seasonings and cover. Cook 1 hour over very low heat. Add potatoes and 1/2 cup water, if needed. Cover and cook 1/2 hour over very low heat.

For a variation: transfer mixture to a baking dish and top with rich biscuits. Place in hot oven at 425 F until biscuits are toasty brown.

BASIC BAKING MIX

Makes about 4 cups.
 To vary the baking mix, you can replace half of the all-purpose flour with whole-wheat flour or cornmeal.

2 3/4 cups all-purpose flour
1/3 cup nonfat dry milk powder
1 tablespoon sugar
1 tablespoon baking powder
1 teaspoon salt
6 tablespoons solid vegetable shortening.

Combine flour, dry milk, sugar, baking powder, salt and shortening in food processor. Pulse until mixture is well blended and smooth.

Store in container with tight-fitting cover in cool place for up to 4 weeks. Stir well before using.

SALMON PIE

1 can (about 7 ounces) salmon
1 cup thawed frozen peas
2 green onions, sliced
3/4 cup shredded Muenster cheese
2 eggs
1 cup low-fat milk
2/3 cup Basic Baking Mix
1/4 cup dill sprigs
1/4 teaspoon each salt and pepper

Preheat oven to 400 degrees. Coat inside of 9-inch pie plate with nonstick cooking spray. Drain salmon; remove skin and bones. Coarsely flake. Combine with peas, green onion and cheese. Spread evenly in prepared pie plate. Blend eggs, milk, baking mix, dill, salt and pepper in blender or processor. Pour over mixture in pie plate and then bake in preheated 400 degree oven 25 to 30 minutes until browned on top and fork inserted in center comes out clean. Let stand a few minutes and then cut into wedges. Serves 6.

CHICKEN PIE

1 medium-size onion, chopped
2 teaspoons vegetable oil
1 package (10 ounces) frozen chopped broccoli, thawed
1 cup chopped cooked chicken
1 cup shredded Swiss cheese
2 eggs
1 cup low-fat milk
2/3 cup Basic Baking Mix (Recipe on Page 62)
1 teaspoon prepared mustard
1/2 teaspoon each salt and thyme
1/4 teaspoon pepper

Preheat oven to 400 degrees. Coat inside of 9-inch pie plate with nonstick cooking spray. Saute onion in oil in nonstick skillet until tender. Combine broccoli, chicken, cheese and onion; spread evenly over bottom of prepared pie plate.

Blend eggs, milk, baking mix, mustard, salt, thyme and pepper in blender or processor. Pour over chicken mixture.

Bake in 400 degree oven 30 to 35 minutes until browned on top and knife inserted in center comes out clean. Cool 5 minutes. Cut into wedges. Makes 6 servings.

FIVE-HOUR STEW

2 pounds stew meat
1 green pepper, cut into pieces
4 large Idaho potatoes, cut into pieces
6 carrots, cut into pieces
1 20-ounce can of tomatoes
3 onions, cut into small pieces
2 teaspoons salt
1 tablespoon sugar
5 heaping teaspoons tapioca
Celery to taste, cut finely

Mix all ingredients together and put into a large baking dish or casserole. Cover and bake in oven for 5 hours at 250 degrees. Do not open cover during the cooking period. This recipe can be made in two 2-quart casseroles. Freezes well. Delicious when warmed over. I normally use beef for stew meat, but have also used elk and deer meat and this is an excellent stew to fix when you're busy because you don't have to tend it all the time.

Courtesy Carolyn Stauduhar, Stevensville, Montana

CURRIED HAM ROLL-UPS

1 pkg. (6 oz.) sliced cooked ham
1 pkg (10 oz.) frozen broccoli spears
1 tablespoon butter
2 tablespoons all-purpose flour
1/2 teaspoon salt
1/4 teaspoon curry powder
1/4 teaspoon onion powder
Dash white pepper
1 cup skim milk
Paprika

Separate ham slices and set aside. Cook broccoli according to package directions, just until barely tender. Drain well and divide evenly between ham slices. Roll ham around broccoli and then place rolls, seam side down, in shallow baking dish; set aside. Melt butter in small saucepan. Remove from heat and stir in flour and seasonings until smooth; then stir in skim milk. Cook over medium heat with constant stirring until sauce is bubbly. Pour sauce over ham rolls and bake uncovered at 350 degrees for 25 to 30 minutes. Sprinkle with paprika before serving. Makes 4 to 6 servings.

WILD RICE AND CHICKEN

1 package (6 ounces) long grain & wild rice
1/4 cup butter or margarine
1/3 cup chopped onion
1/3 cup flour
1 teaspoon salt
Dash black pepper
1 cup half and half
1 cup chicken broth
2 cups cubed cooked chicken
1/3 cup chopped pimiento
1/3 cup chopped parsley
1/4 cup chopped almonds

Prepare contents of rice and seasoning packets according to package directions. Meanwhile, melt butter in large saucepan. Add onion and cook over low heat until tender. Stir in flour, salt and pepper. Gradually stir in half and half and chicken broth. Cook, stirring constantly, until thickened. Stir in chicken, pimiento, parsley, almonds and cooked rice. Place in 2-quart casserole. Bake, uncovered, in 425 degree oven for 30 minutes. Makes 6 to 8 servings.

DESSERTS

UPSIDE DOWN
GERMAN CHOCOLATE CAKE

Frosting:
1 1/4 cups water
1/4 cup margarine or butter
1 cup firmly packed brown sugar
1 cup coconut
1 cup miniature marshmallows
1 cup chopped nuts

Cake:
4-ounce bar German sweet chocolate
1/2 cup water
2 1/2 cups all purpose flour
1 1/2 cups sugar
1 teaspoon soda
1/2 teaspoon salt
1 cup dairy sour cream
1/2 cup margarine or butter, softened
1 teaspoon vanilla
3 eggs

Heat oven to 350 degrees. In small saucepan, heat 1 1/4 cups water and 1/4 cup margarine until margarine melts. Pour into ungreased 13 x 9-inch pan. Stir in brown sugar and coconut; sprinkle marshmallows and nuts over top.

In saucepan over low heat, melt chocolate with 1/2 cup water. Lightly spoon flour into measuring cup; level off. In large bowl, combine chocolate mixture with remaining cake ingredients. Beat 3 minutes at medium speed. Carefully spoon batter over coconut-marshmallow mixture. (Place pan on foil or cookie sheet during baking to guard against spillage.) Bake at 350 degrees for 40 to 50 minutes or until toothpick inserted in center comes out clean. Serve inverted onto serving plate. Refrigerate leftovers.

OATMEAL CAKE & FROSTING

1 cup quick oats
1/2 cup butter
1 1/4 cups boiling water
2 eggs, well beaten
1 cup sugar
1 teaspoon vanilla
1 1/2 cups flour
1/2 teaspoon allspice
1/2 teaspoon salt
1/4 teaspoon cloves
1 teaspoon soda
1 teaspoon cinnamon
1/2 teaspoon ginger

Combine oats, butter and boiling water. Set aside for 20 minutes. Beat together eggs, sugar and vanilla. Sift dry ingredients and add, along with oats, to sugar mixture. Beat well. Pour into greased 13 x 9 inch baking pan. Bake at 350 degrees for 30 to 35 minutes. Allow to cool.

Frosting:
1/2 cup brown sugar
1/4 cup melted butter
3 tablespoons milk
3/4 cup coconut
1/3 cup chopped nuts

Combine frosting ingredients. Spread on cake and place under the broiler for 1 minute or until frosting begins to bubble.

CARROT CAKE AND TOPPING

1 1/4 cups salad oil
2 cups white sugar
2 1/3 cups sifted flour
2 teaspoons baking powder
1 teaspoon soda
1 teaspoon salt
2 teaspoons cinnamon
4 eggs
3 cups grated raw carrots
1/2 cup nuts

Add dry ingredients alternately with eggs, then add raw carrots. Pour into well greased and floured 13 x 9 inch pan. Bake at 350 degrees for 35 minutes.

Topping:
1 cup white sugar
1/4 cup cornstarch
1 cup orange juice
1 teaspoon lemon juice.

Combine these ingredients. After they have cooked and thickened, add:

2 tablespoons orange rind
2 tablespoons butter

Spread on cake while hot.

FRESH APPLE CAKE

2 or 3 apples
1 cup sugar
1 1/2 cups flour
1 teaspoon baking soda
1/2 teaspoon salt
1 teaspoon cinnamon
1/2 teaspoon nutmeg
1/2 teaspoon allspice
1/2 cup melted butter
1 egg
1/2 cup raisins
1/2 cup chopped walnuts

Peel and core apples. Chop coarsely and measure 1 3/4 cups into large bowl. Add sugar and spices and let stand 10 minutes. Blend melted butter and beaten egg into apple mixture. Sift flour and soda and blend into first mixture. Add raisins and nuts. Bake in greased loaf pan for 45 to 50 minutes at 350 degrees.

LEMON LOAF CAKE

1 pkg. yellow cake mix
1 pkg. lemon jello (dry)
2/3 cup oil or corn oil
2/3 cup water
4 whole eggs (not beaten)

Place the ingredients in a large bowl and beat until smooth. Then pour into a greased and floured cake pan. Bake 1 hour in 325 degree oven. Let set for about a half an hour before taking out of pan.

RED DEVILS FOOD CAKE

Sift together into bowl:
1 2/3 cups sifted flour
1 1/2 cups sugar
1 1/4 teaspoons soda
1 teaspoon salt
1/2 cup cocoa
Add:
1/2 cup soft shortening
1 cup milk
1 teaspoon vanilla

Beat for 2 minutes and then add 3 eggs and beat 2 more minutes. Pour into greased pan 9 x 13 inches and bake at 350 degrees for 45 minutes.

DEVILS FOOD CAKE
SALAD DRESSING VARIATION

2 cups all purpose flour
1 cup sugar
5 heaping tablespoons cocoa
2 teaspoons soda

Sift above together. Then add:
1 cup salad dressing
1 cup water
1 teaspoon vanilla

Mix thoroughly and bake in greased layer pans at 350 degrees for 30 minutes.

Frosting:
Bring to full rolling boil and boil for a second:
1/3 cup milk
1/4 cup butter or margarine
Remove from heat and add:
1 6 ounce package chocolate bits
1 teaspoon vanilla
1 handful small marshmallows
Leave until melted. Stir in: 2 1/4 cups powdered sugar and frost cake.

ZUCCHINI CAKE

1/2 cup margarine
1/2 cup oil
1 3/4 cups sugar
2 eggs
1 teaspoon vanilla
1/2 teaspoon baking powder
1 teaspoon soda
1/2 cup sour cream
2 1/2 cups flour
4 tablespoons cocoa
1/2 teaspoon cinnamon
1/2 teaspoon cloves
1/2 cup chocolate chips
2 cups shredded raw zucchini

Combine margarine, oil and sugar. Then add eggs, vanilla and sour cream. Add remaining ingredients, except chocolate chips. Pour in 2 (8 inch) loaf pans that have been greased and floured. Sprinkle chocolate chips on top. Bake at 325 degrees 35 to 40 minutes.

STREUSEL FILLED COFFEE CAKE

Filling and topping:
1/2 cup brown sugar
2 teaspoons cinnamon
2 tablespoons flour
2 tablespoons melted butter
1/2 cup chopped nuts

Mix together with fork before mixing coffee cake.

Coffee cake:
1 1/2 cups sifted flour
3 teaspoons baking powder
1/4 teaspoon salt
3/4 cup sugar
1/4 cup shortening
1 egg
1 teaspoon vanilla
1/2 cup milk

Sift dry ingredients, cut in shortening. Blend in well beaten egg mixed with milk. Spread 1/2 the batter in greased and floured pan. Sprinkle with 1/2 the streusel mixture. Add the other 1/2 of the batter and sprinkle with remaining streusel mixture. Bake at 375 degrees, 25 to 30 minutes.

MONTANA HUCKLEBERRY PIE

3 cups huckleberries
3/4 cup sugar
3 tablespoons flour

Mix and cook over medium heat until thick. Pour into prepared pie shell, dot with butter. Bake at 375 degrees for one hour.

Courtesy Marianne Roose, Fortine, Montana

HUCKLEBERRY PIE

2 cups huckleberries
Sugar
Corn starch

Use double crust.

Boil huckleberries in water, to cover about 2 inches.

Add 1/2 cup sugar to 2 cups berries. Mix 1 part corn starch to 3 parts water. Add to the berries, stirring until thick. 1 tablespoon lemon is optional.

Courtesy Doris Glass, Clinton, Montana

CHOCOLATE PETAL CRUST

1/2 cup butter or margarine
1 cup sugar
1 egg
1 teaspoon vanilla
1 1/4 cups unsifted all-purpose flour
1/2 cup cocoa
3/4 teaspoon baking soda
1/4 teaspoon salt

Cream butter or margarine, sugar, egg and vanilla until light and fluffy. Combine flour, cocoa, baking soda and salt and add these to creamed mixture. Shape soft dough into two 1 1/2 inch rolls. Wrap in waxed paper and chill until firm. Cut one roll into 1/8-inch slices; arrange, edges touching, on bottom and sides of greased 9-inch pie pan. Small spaces in crust will not affect pie.) Bake at 375 degrees for 8 to 10 minutes. Cool.

NEVER-FAIL PIE CRUST

4 - 4 1/2 cups unbleached flour, sifted
1 tablespoon sugar
3 teaspoons salt
1 egg
1 tablespoon vinegar
1/2 cup water
1 3/4 cups shortening

Sift the flour, sugar and salt into a large bowl. Beat the egg and combine with vinegar and water. Cut the shortening into the flour, sprinkle with the egg mixture, and mix all together. Gather the dough into a ball, wrap in waxed paper and chill for about 30 minutes before using. This dough can be kept refrigerated up to 1 week, or you can divide it into 4 parts (1 pie shell each), wrap each securely, and freeze until ready to use. Makes four 9" pie shells.

To make the shell: Turn 1/4 of the dough on a floured board and roll to fit a 9" pie pan. (Remember to allow for the sides and leave a little over besides.) Fold it in half, gently lift into the pan, and with your fingers, fit the dough without stretching. Trim the edge slightly larger than the outer rim of the pan, and flute.

If the recipe calls for a baked shell: Prick the bottom and sides of the shell with a fork and bake for 12 to 15 minutes in a preheated 450 degree oven, or until golden. Cool before adding the filling.

Or a partially baked shell: Bake the shell in a preheated 450 degree oven for 5 minutes; then cool.

To prevent a soggy bottom in a juicy pie: Chill the unbaked pie shell for 15 minutes before making the filling. Add the filling just before baking. Or, you also can bake the bottom crust for 10 minutes in a preheated 450 degree oven before adding the filling.

CINNAMON ROLLS

1 package yeast
1/4 cup water
1 cup milk, scalded
1/4 cup sugar
1/4 cup shortening
1 teaspoon salt
3 1/2 cups sifted flour
1 egg

Soften yeast in warm water (about 110 degrees). Combine milk, sugar, shortening and salt; cool to lukewarm. Add 1 cup of the flour and beat well. Beat in yeast and egg. Gradually add remaining flour to form soft dough. Cover and let rise in warm (about 80 degrees) place until double in size (usually 1 1/2 to 2 hours). On a lightly floured surface, roll one-half of the recipe to a rectangle about 16 inches long. Spread 1/4 cup soft margarine or butter over dough, sprinkle with 1/2 cup sugar and 1 1/2 teaspoons cinnamon, 1/4 cup raisins. Roll lengthwise. Cut in 1 inch slices. Place cut sides down in greased 9x9x2-inch pan. Cover and let rise until double (usually 30 to 40 minutes). Then bake at 375 degrees (about 20 to 25 minutes). Remove from pan and frost with powdered sugar icing. Makes 14 to 16 rolls and a great treat whether at home or in the camp. Repeat with remaining one-half of dough.

Courtesy Patricia Burk, Stevensville, Montana

GRAHAM CRACKER CRUST

1 cup crushed graham crackers
1/4 cup butter or margarine
1/4 cup sugar

Blend together crushed crackers, sugar and butter. Line a 9-inch pan. Bake at 375 degrees for 8 to 10 minutes. Cool.

APPLE PIE

5 cups sliced apples (5 medium)
1 cup sugar
2 tablespoons flour
1/2 teaspoon cinnamon
1/4 teaspoon nutmeg (optional)
2 tablespoons butter or margarine
1 crust for double-crust pie (Recipes on Pages 76-77)

Roll half of the pie crust to fit an 8 or 9 inch pie shell. Arrange apple slices in crust and sprinkle with mixture of sugar, flour, cinnamon, nutmeg. Dot with butter or margarine. Arrange top crust; crimp edges securely, moistening with a little water, if necessary. Bake at 400 degrees for 60 minutes. Makes one pie.

PEAR CRUNCH PIE

1/4 cup sugar
2 tablespoons cornstarch
1/8 teaspoon salt
1/8 teaspoon nutmeg
1 can (1 pound 13 ounces) pear halves
1 tablespoon lemon juice
1 tablespoon butter
1 9-inch pie shell, unbaked (Recipes on Pages 76-77)

Topping:
1 cup oatmeal
1/3 cup brown sugar
1/3 cup butter or margarine, melted
1/3 cup chopped pecans
1/4 teaspoon nutmeg
1/4 teaspoon cinnamon

In saucepan, combine first 4 ingredients. Drain pears, but keep liquid in small jar or pitcher. Add water to reserved liquid to make 1 1/2 cups and then stir liquid into saucepan. Cook over medium heat, stirring constantly until mixture is thick and clear. Remove from heat and stir in lemon juice and butter. Slice pears and arrange in unbaked pie shell. Pour sauce mixture over pears. Combine topping ingredients and sprinkle over pie. Bake at 425 degrees for 20 to 25 minutes.

RASPBERRY PIE

1 Graham Cracker Pie Shell (Recipe on Page 77)
1 package raspberry Jello
1 1/4 cup hot water
1 pint vanilla ice cream
1 1/2 cups of raspberries

Dissolve the package of Jello in hot water. Slowly add ice cream, stirring until melted, chill until thickened but not set, then stir the fruit in gently. Pour mixture into a graham cracker pie shell and chill until firm.

Courtesy Sonny Templeton, Lincoln, Montana

BANANA CREAM PIE

1 package vanilla pudding or pie filling mix (4 serving size)
Milk
1 baked 8-inch pastry shell (Recipes on Pages 76-77)
3-4 ripe bananas

Prepare pudding mix according to package directions for pie filling; cool 5 to 10 minutes. Fill pie shell with alternate layers of filling and sliced bananas, starting and ending with cream mixture. Refrigerate. Garnish with additional banana slices and sweetened whipped cream. Makes one pie.

CHERRY PIE

1 Graham cracker crust (Recipe on Page 77)
1 8-ounce package cream cheese, softened
1/2 teaspoon vanilla
1 21-ounce can cherry pie filling
1 20-ounce can crushed pineapple, well drained
1 cup heavy cream
1/4 cup confectioners' sugar

Combine cheese, vanilla and 2 tablespoons pie filling, mixing thoroughly until well blended. Stir in 1/4 cup well drained pineapple and 1/2 cup pie filling. Beat cream and gradually add sugar until soft peaks form. Fold into cream cheese mixture. Pour into crust. Top with remaining pineapple and pie filling. Chill until firm.

BUTTERSCOTCH LEMON PIE

1 cup boiling water
1 3-ounce package lemon flavor gelatin
1/4 teaspoon salt
3 eggs
1 6-ounce package (1 cup) butterscotch morsels
1 9-inch prepared Graham cracker pie shell
Whipped cream

In small bowl, combine boiling water, gelatin and salt. Stir until gelatin is dissolved. Set this bowl aside. Then, using a blender container, process eggs at medium speed for 2 minutes. Add butterscotch morsels and lemon gelatin mixture; blend until smooth. Set aside about 5 minutes and then pour into prepared pie shell. Chill about 2 hours or until firm. Garnish with whipped cream. Makes one pie.

GREEN APPLE PIE

6 tart green apples
2/3 cup sugar
1/8 teaspoon nutmeg
1/8 teaspoon salt
2 tablespoons dried currants
1/4 teaspoon cinnamon
1/4 teaspoon ginger
1 tablespoon corn flakes
1 1/2 tablespoons butter
1 recipe pastry (Recipes on Pages 76-77)

Peel, core and cut the apples into thin slices. Combine and spread all the dry ingredients over the apples, and let stand 15 to 20 minutes. Place this filling in pastry lined pie dish. Dot with butter. Dampen edge; put the top crust on; seal and flute. Slash the top crust to let out steam during baking. Bake in a preheated oven at 450 degrees for 10 minutes, then reduce heat to 350 degrees and bake for about 45 minutes.

STRAWBERRY PIE

8 ounces strawberry glaze
1 1/2 pints fresh strawberries
1 9-inch pre-baked pie shell (Recipes on Pages 76-77)
Whipped topping

Wash berries, remove stems and drain carefully. Pour glaze over berries in mixing bowl and tumble gently with a spoon until berries are coated. Pour glazed berries into pie shell and smooth out to the edges. Refrigerate or cool one hour before serving. Excellent with ice cream or whipped cream.

PEACH PIE

1 9" unbaked pie shell **(Recipes on Pages 76-77)**
3/4 cup sugar
1 tablespoon cornstarch
2 tablespoons tapioca
1/4 teaspoon salt
1 quart fresh peeled, sliced peaches
1/4 cup lemon juice
1/4 teaspoon grated nutmeg
Crumb topping **(Recipe on Page 88)**

Combine sugar, cornstarch, tapioca and salt. Mix thoroughly with peaches and lemon juice. Spoon peach mixture into prepared pie shell and sprinkle with nutmeg. Cover with crumb topping. Bake in preheated 425 degree oven 40 to 50 minutes, or until bubbly and lightly browned.

RAISIN SOUR CREAM PIE

3/4 cup sugar
2 tablespoons cornstarch
1/4 teaspoon salt
2 eggs, beaten
2 cups sour cream
1 cup raisins
2 tablespoons lemon juice
1 baked 9-inch pie shell **(Recipes on Pages 76-77)**

In top of double boiler, blend together sugar, cornstarch and salt. Combine with beaten eggs, 1 1/2 cups sour cream, raisins and lemon juice. Cook and stir over hot water until thick. Pour into baked pie shell. When cool, top with remaining 1/2 cup sour cream. Chill several hours before serving.

BANANA CHOCOLATE PIE

1 1/4 cups crushed Graham crackers
1/2 cup crushed chocolate fudge sandwich cookies
1 package chocolate pudding and pie filling mix
1 package vanilla pudding and pie filling mix
1 1/2 teaspoons gelatin (to be added to each filling)
1 large banana

Crush grahams and chocolate fudge sandwich cookies to a fine consistency. In a medium mixing bowl combine crumbs and melted butter. Stir with a fork. Press in bottom and up sides of a 9-inch pie pan. Combine gelatin with dry pudding mixes, half with the chocolate, half with the vanilla. Prepare puddings according to package directions. Cool to room temperature. Place one layer of sliced bananas on bottom of pie crust. Pour chocolate filling over bananas. Next, pour vanilla filling over the chocolate. Top with remaining bananas just before serving. Cool until ready to serve.

HERSHEY BAR PIE

1 Hershey's Milk Chocolate Bar or Milk Chocolate with Almonds Bar (1/2 pound)
1/3 cup milk
1 1/2 cups miniature or 15 regular marshmallows
1 cup heavy cream
Chocolate Petal Crust (Recipe on Page 77)

Prepare pie shell and set aside. Break Hershey bar, chopping almonds into small pieces. Then melt the bar with milk in top of double boiler over hot water. Add marshmallows, stirring until melted; cool completely. Whip cream until stiff and then fold into chocolate mixture. Pour into crust. Chill several hours until firm. Garnish with whipped topping or chilled cherry pie filling. A tasty, rich dessert that serves 8.

FRESH LEMON MERINGUE PIE

1 1/2 cups sugar
1/4 cup plus 2 tablespoons cornstarch
1/4 teaspoon salt
1/2 cup cold water
1/2 cup fresh squeezed lemon juice
3 egg yolks
2 tablespoons butter or margarine
1 1/2 cups boiling water
1 teaspoon fresh grated lemon peel
Few drops of yellow food coloring (optional)
1 (9-inch) baked pie shell (Recipes on Pages 76-77)
Meringue (see recipe below)

In saucepan, thoroughly combine sugar, cornstarch and salt. Gradually stir in cold water and lemon juice. Blend in egg yolks. Add butter and boiling water. Bring to full boil over medium-high heat, stirring constantly. Reduce heat to medium and boil 1 minute. Remove from heat and then stir in lemon peel and food coloring. Pour into pie shell. Top with meringue, sealing well at edges. Bake at 350 degrees for 12 to 15 minutes or until browned.

MERINGUE

3 egg whites
1/4 teaspoon cream of tartar
6 tablespoons sugar

Beat egg whites until foamy; add cream of tartar and continue beating to soft peak stage. Gradually add sugar, beating until egg whites are stiff but not dry.

PUMPKIN PIE

2 slightly beaten eggs
1 1/2 cups canned or cooked, sieved pumpkin
1 cup sugar
1/2 teaspoon salt
1 teaspoon cinnamon
1/4 teaspoon cloves
1/4 teaspoon nutmeg
1 2/3 cups undiluted evaporated milk
9-inch single-crust unbaked pie shell **(Recipes on Pages 76-77)**

Combine eggs, pumpkin, sugar, salt and spices, and gradually pour in evaporated milk. Mix well and then pour into unbaked pie shell. Bake in hot oven (425 degrees) 15 minutes or so and then reduce to 375 degrees and continue baking about 40 minutes, or until fork inserted near center of pie comes out clean. Cool before serving. Some like to serve with whipped cream.

SIMPLE PLUM CREAM PIE

1 package (8 ounces) cream cheese, slightly softened
1/2 cup light corn syrup
1 cup cold milk
1 package (3 3/4 ounces) instant vanilla pudding mix
1 9-inch Graham cracker crust (Recipe on Page 77)
1 cup pitted, sliced ripe fresh plums
1/4 cup red currant jelly, melted

With mixer at high speed beat cream cheese until smooth. Gradually beat in corn syrup until light and fluffy. Set aside. With mixer at lowest speed, beat milk and pudding mix 2 minutes. Fold in cheese mixture and then immediately spoon into crust. Refrigerate or cool until set. Arrange plums on top of pie. Brush fruit with jelly. Makes 6 servings.

PECAN PIE

Pastry for 9-inch one-crust pie
8-ounce package cream cheese, softened
1/3 cup sugar
1/4 teaspoon salt
1 teaspoon vanilla
1 egg
1 1/4 cups chopped pecans

Topping:
3 eggs
1/4 cup sugar
1 cup light or dark corn syrup
1 teaspoon vanilla

Heat oven to 375 degrees. Prepare pastry. In small bowl, combine cream cheese, 1/3 cup sugar, salt, 1 teaspoon vanilla and 1 egg and then beat at medium speed until well blended. Spread in bottom of pastry-lined pan and sprinkle with pecans. In small bowl, combine all topping ingredients; beat on medium speed just until blended. Pour topping over pecans. Bake at 375 degrees for 35 to 40 minutes or until center is firm. Serves 8.

BERRY PIE

1 1/2 tablespoons corn starch
1 cup sugar
4 cups fresh blueberries or strawberries, cut in half
Double crust pastry for 9-inch pie (Recipes on Pages 76-77)

Mix corn starch and sugar and, using large spoon, toss with berries. Turn into pastry lined pie plate. Cover pie with pastry and seal and flute edge. Cut several slits in top crust to permit escape of steam. Bake in 425 degree oven 35 to 45 minutes or until browned.

SUPREME PECAN PIE

3 eggs
1 cup light or dark corn syrup
1 cup sugar
2 tablespoons margarine, melted
1 teaspoon vanilla
1/8 teaspoon salt
1 to 1 1/2 cups pecans
1 unbaked (9-inch) pastry shell (**Recipes on Pages 76-77**)

In medium bowl with mixer at medium speed beat eggs slightly. Beat in corn syrup, sugar, margarine, vanilla and salt. Stir in pecans. Pour filling into pastry shell. Bake in 350 degree oven 55 to 65 minutes or until toothpick inserted halfway between center and edge comes out clean. Cool. Some like to serve pie with whipped cream.

GRASSHOPPER PIE

Crust:
1 1/2 cups filled chocolate cookie crumbs (about 20 cookies)
1/4 cup butter or margarine, melted

Filling:
1 envelope unflavored gelatin
1/3 cup cold water
1 cup chilled whipping cream or 1 envelope whipped topping mix
1 cup vanilla pudding
1/4 cup white creme de cocoa
1/4 cup green creme de menthe

Crush cookies, add melted butter and mix thoroughly. Press firmly to bottom and sides of 9" pie pan. Chill. Then, in a small saucepan, sprinkle gelatin on water to soften. Stir over low heat until gelatin is dissolved. Whip cream or whip topping according to directions on package. Blend pudding, cream and liqueurs, fold in gelatin. Pour into crumb crust. Chill several hours.

CRUMB TOPPING

1/3 cup firmly packed light brown sugar
1/4 cup all purpose flour
1/2 teaspoon cinnamon
3 tablespoons slightly softened butter

Combine brown sugar, flour and cinnamon. Blend in butter with pastry blender, fork or fingers until mixture is crumbly.

PEACH COBBLER

12 peaches
1 cup sugar
1 egg
1 tablespoon melted butter
1 cup flour
1 teaspoon baking powder
1/4 cup milk

Spread peaches in bottom of 8x12-inch pan (if fresh peaches are used add 3/4 cup sugar). Spread cake mixture over peaches and bake 45 minutes at 350 degrees.

RHUBARB DESSERT

4 cups rhubarb
1 cup sugar
1 package white or yellow cake mix
3 1/2-ounce package strawberry Jello
A layer of miniature marshmallows

Slice rhubarb into pieces about 1 inch long. Put in moderate-sized cake pan with sugar, jello and marshmallows. Mix cake as directed on package and pour over the top. Bake at 350 degrees for 45 minutes.

APPLE CRISP

4 cups sliced apples
1/2 cup water
1 teaspoon cinnamon
7 tablespoons butter
1 cup brown or white sugar
3/4 cup flour

Put apples in buttered dish, add water and cinnamon, work other ingredients together until crumbly and spread over apple mixture. Bake uncovered in moderate oven (350 degrees) 35 to 40 minutes. Serve with whipped cream for added touch.

EASY CHERRY SUPREME

1/4 cup butter or margarine
1/2 cup flour
1/2 cup sugar
1 teaspoon baking powder
1/4 teaspoon salt
1/2 cup milk
1 can cherry pie filling

Melt butter in a 1 1/2 quart casserole. Blend flour, sugar, baking powder, salt and milk. Pour mixture over melted butter. Do not stir. Pour pie filling evenly over the mixture but do not stir. Bake at 350 degrees for 45-50 minutes.

DOUGHNUTS

1 cup sugar
1/2 cup sweet cream
1 egg
1 cup cultured sour cream
1/2 teaspoon salt
2 teaspoons soda
2 teaspoons nutmeg
Flour for soft dough (approximately 3 1/2 cups)

Combine ingredients and mix thoroughly. Roll to 1/4 inch thick. Cut and fry in medium hot safflower oil. Makes about 3 dozen small doughnuts.

RAISED POTATO DOUGHNUTS

Cream these ingredients:
1/2 cup shortening, melted
1 1/2 cups mashed potatoes
1/4 cup sugar

Dissolve in 2 cups cooled scaled milk:
2 packages yeast
6 cups flour
1 teaspoon salt

Mix all ingredients and let rise for one-half hour. Roll out and cut. Then let rise again before frying in deep fat.

BUTTERSCOTCH COOKIES

4 cups brown sugar
1 cup lard
7 cups flour
4 eggs, unbeaten
1 tablespoon soda
1 tablespoon cream of tartar

Mix well. Shape into rolls, wrap in oiled paper and chill. Slice thin and bake in hot oven.

CAKE COOKIES

1 package chocolate cake mix
3 eggs
1/3 cup oil

Mix all ingredients together and drop by teaspoonsful on ungreased cookie sheet. Bake at 375 degrees for 8 to 10 minutes.

PEANUT BUTTER COOKIES

1 cup sugar
1 cup peanut butter
1 egg

Mix all ingredients together, spoon a heaping tablespoon of batter onto lightly greased metal cookie sheet and bake at 350 degrees for 8 to 10 minutes.

SOFT MOLASSES COOKIES

3/4 cup shortening
3/4 cup brown sugar
3/4 cup molasses
2 eggs (beaten)
3/4 cup buttermilk (or other sour milk)
2 teaspoons soda dissolved in buttermilk
1 teaspoon salt
2 cups flour
1 teaspoon nutmeg
1 1/2 teaspoons ginger

Dissolve 2 teaspoons soda in buttermilk to begin. Then add spices and salt to 2 cups flour and stir into above mixture. Add enough flour to make soft dough. Chill and roll to about 1/4 inch thickness. Cut with cookie cutters. Bake on greased baking sheet 12 to 15 minutes at 350 degrees. Good with just sugar sprinkled on dough when rolled out or with plain powdered sugar frosting. This is my favorite Christmas cookie. Makes about 5 dozen.

Courtesy Lena Jane Bacon

CHOCOLATE BROWNIES

1/2 cup butter
1 cup sugar
2 beaten eggs
1/2 cup nuts
1/2 cup cocoa
3/4 cup flour
1/2 cup milk
3/4 teaspoon vanilla

Cream butter and sugar, add eggs and beat until fluffy. Sift cocoa and flour and add alternately with milk. Add nuts and bake at 350 degrees for 30 to 35 minutes. Frost with chocolate powdered sugar frosting or cut in squares. Sprinkle lightly with powdered sugar .

MOLASSES GINGER COOKIES

Mix together thoroughly:
1/3 cup soft shortening
1 cup brown sugar
1 1/2 cups dark molasses
1/2 cup cold water

Sift together and stir in:
6 cups sifted flour
1 teaspoon salt
1 teaspoon allspice
1 teaspoon ginger
1 teaspoon cloves
1 teaspoon cinnamon

Then stir in 2 teaspoons soda dissolved in 3 tablespoons cold water. Chill dough and roll out to about 1/2 inch thickness. Then cut with a round cutter about the size of the lid on a mustard jar. Place far apart on lightly greased baking sheet and bake 15 to 20 minutes at about 350 degrees, or until no imprint remains on a cookie when you tap it with a finger.

NORWEGIAN COOKIES

1 pound butter
1 pound flour - 4 cups, sifted
1/2 pound powdered sugar (equals 1 3/4 cups)
4 hard boiled egg yolks
4 uncooked egg yolks

Sift flour in heap in bowl. Mash egg yolks (or rub through strainer). Add raw egg yolks, one at a time. Add sugar to egg mixture. Put butter on flour and then egg mixture. Mix thoroughly. Bake in 350 degree oven. The dough should be squeezed through a cookie press and then shaped by hand into a small ring. Makes several dozen.

GERMAN CHOCOLATE
CREAM CHEESE BROWNIES

Brownie Layer:
1 package (4 ounces) German sweet chocolate
1/4 cup margarine
3/4 cup sugar
2 eggs
1 teaspoon vanilla
1/2 cup all-purpose flour
1/2 cup chopped nuts

Cream Cheese Topping:
4 ounces cream cheese, softened
1/4 cup sugar
1 egg
1 tablespoon all-purpose flour

Brownie Layer:
Melt chocolate and margarine in 2-quart saucepan over very low heat, or in double-boiler, stirring constantly until melted. Stir sugar into melted chocolate. Stir in eggs and vanilla until completely mixed. Mix in flour until well blended. Stir in nuts. Spread in greased 8-inch square pan.

Cream Cheese Topping:
Mix cream cheese, sugar, egg and flour until smooth. Spoon over brownie mixture; swirl with knife or spatula to firm up.

Bake at 350 degrees for 35 minutes or until wooden pick inserted in center comes out almost clean. (Do not overbake.) Cool in pan, cut into squares. Makes 12 to 16 brownies.

BIG FISH IN THE FRYING PAN

It wasn't until the summer of my eighth year that I came to a lifelong determination about fish no matter how they're fixed, though up to that time and since I've eaten them many times. It's just that each time I see or smell them frying, I'm reminded of a meal of freshly-caught trout my mother fixed on a Fourth of July family camping-fishing trip and my stomach gets, well, a bit queasy....

There's good reason for that, too, when you've learned even earlier in life, like around six or seven, that fishing and the art of trying for the big ones is going to be a way of life with you. For me, it became that way shortly after my Dad turned me loose to fish on my own, which came to pass somewhere in that six or seven year range, I'm not sure.

By that rainy Holiday weekend of which I speak, however, all my family knew that when we went fishing, even in small creeks for brook trout that seldom got big, I was off by myself, seeking out the deep holes and undercut banks where the promise of a big fish was found. It was so on that rainy, cold early-summer weekend when our family went deep into the woods to a place known as Trixie Dam on Good Creek in heavily-timbered country of northwestern Montana.

In those days the road to Trixie Dam was but a pair of tracks in the mud, almost impassable and made actually so by a big mud-hole about a quarter of a mile from the site where we set up camp above the old wooden dam, which had been constructed and used to provide spring runoff water for log drives on the Stillwater River in the early days of logging in that country. Even then, in the mid Forties, only remnants of the long out-of-use dam remained but upstream from it lay long, deep, cold runs of the kind of clear water big brook trout loved and though the willow-infested bottom made access difficult for a boy like me, I was off to the creek shortly after daylight that first morning, by myself, trying for a big fish while most everyone else was content to pursue smaller brookies for the frying pan.

Now I got the smaller ones, too, and like everyone else I put them on a willow stringer to take back to camp later. But sometime in midafternoon, my persistence and hard work paid off. A brook trout of magnificent proportions slashed out from under a deeply-cut bank and took my red-beaded spinner and angleworm. Subsequently, the fishing battle of the century, in my mind at least, ensued. The brightly-colored fish ran long and deep and thrashed wildly as he tried to throw my hook; up to my chest in the water, my back against the stabbing willows, I played him on my prized telescoping metal rod as best I could. And, finally, maybe a half an hour after I'd hooked him, my trophy came to my grip (we had no such things as nets in those days — those were fancy things that city fishermen used) and he was mine.

I was a mile or more upstream from camp when I caught the fish and all I could think of was getting him back to camp, to show him to my Mom and Dad and measure him. I crashed through the willows, sloshing out through the brush of the flooded bottomland to get to higher ground and then race back to camp with my fish.

My Dad and my uncle Frank (Frank Graves), home on furlough from the Army and, to me, a hero freshly home from the wars in Europe and the invasion of Germany where he'd been among the first of Patton's troops to go into Germany, were fishing at the dam right below camp. They came running to my excited calls about a "big fish." Mom, I learned, wasn't there. She had walked back to the car to get a sack of potatoes and some cans of pork and beans for dinner. Dad and Uncle Frank were as excited as I was about my fish and they laid him out on a rock and Dad pulled a cloth measuring tape from his jacket. "This is like the ones we used to catch. Big fish," he said. He stretched the worn tape and pulled it taut and my heart stretched with it. The bright-colored, hook-jawed male brook trout measured twenty-seven and one-quarter inches long. Big fish indeed! It was the biggest brook trout I've ever caught, then or since (in fact, the next closest brookie to it that I've landed was a mere twenty inches long).

Laid out there on that rock, alongside the other fish that we'd caught, most of which were in the eight to ten inch range, with a couple going thirteen or fourteen inches, the trout looked like a monster. "He's a real Leviathan," Uncle Frank said, and even though I didn't know what the word meant then, I agreed with him.

"We need to get a picture," Dad said. He rummaged in the old woodsman's knapsack that he used in those days to carry all his stuff. No camera.

"Must've left the Kodak in the car," he said. "Why don't you run down and get it."

So, off I went on the dead run for the car and the Kodak, which was the name by which all cameras went among the common people back then. Just outside camp I met my Mom and Aunt Clara, coming back from the car with the makings for dinner, and as I went by on the run I shouted something to them about my big fish. But my Mom, like all mothers, just told me to be sure to get back soon because dinner would be ready right away.

I never stopped running and though it took me a few minutes to locate the Kodak in among the pile of stuff in the back seat of our old '37 Ford, it couldn't have taken me more than a half an hour to return to the camp. By then, my Dad and Uncle Frank were back down to the creek, fishing. And Mom, true to her word, was busy over the campfire cooking supper.

I shouted for my Dad as I ran up to the camp and then, when I got to the big, flat rock where we'd laid out my fish, I stopped in disbelief. My fish was gone! I remember stammering to my Dad, "Where's my fish? Where'd you put my fish?"

"It's right there on the rock, with all the rest of them," he shouted from the creek.

But it wasn't. In fact, it and most of the fish that had been on the rock were gone — and we realized instantly, simultaneously, what had happened. Dad came racing up from the creek and we turned to the fire and there, sure enough, in the frying pan, cut up in pieces and covered with flour, its rich, pink flesh already browning and turning crisp in the big frying pan, was my brook trout — the trophy fish of my life, the biggest comparative example of any species of trout I'd caught up to that time or since — reduced, in the practical hands of my mother, to dinner.

I was so shocked I simply walked away and quietly carried the camera back to the car. There was no need for it now. Only later, after everyone else had eaten and the shadows of a wet July evening began to fade into darkness, did I come back for a supper of fried potatoes and beans and to enjoy the warmth of the fire. I wouldn't touch the fried trout, however, and I haven't, really, liked to eat fish much at all from that day to now.

# # # #

MEATS

ROUND STEAK

3/4 cup catsup
1/2 cup Worcestershire sauce
1/3 cup oil
1 teaspoon salt
3-pound boneless beef round steak

In a small bowl combine catsup, Worcestershire, oil, and salt. Place steak in a bowl or doubled plastic bag. Pour mixture over steak, cover or fasten and refrigerate for 24 hours. Then remove steak from marinade and place on a rack over hot charcoal. Grill until done as desired, about 12 minutes on each side for medium, brushing with marinade occasionally. Or, you can place the steak on a rack in a broiler pan. Place under a preheated hot broiler; follow preceding directions for cooking. 6 to 8 servings.

CHUCK STEAK

1/2 cup Teriyaki sauce
1/4 cup water
1/2 teaspoon black pepper
1/2 teaspoon onion powder
2 1/2 pound beef chuck steak, about 1 inch thick
Instant meat tenderizer

Mix together first 4 ingredients and place in a large plastic bag with the steak; press air out and close top securely. Refrigerate 4 to 5 hours, turning occasionally. Remove steak but reserve the marinade. Sprinkle steak with meat tenderizer and pierce surfaces with fork to allow tenderizer to penetrate. Let stand 15 to 20 minutes and then grill 5 to 6 inches from coals for about 6-10 minutes on each side or to desired doneness. Turn and brush with marinade. Makes 4 to 5 servings.

PEPPER STEAK

1 pound round steak (cut in thin strips)
1 cup sliced green pepper
1 cup sliced onion
1/2 cup coarsely chopped celery
1 cup sliced mushrooms
2 tablespoons butter or margarine
1 teaspoon salt
2 tablespoons soy sauce
1 tablespoon corn starch
1 cup water
1 - 1 1/2 teaspoons bay seasoning

In skillet, brown round steak slightly in butter or margarine. Add vegetables, salt and bay seasoning. Stir fry about 5 minutes. Mix corn starch with water and soy sauce. Pour over vegetables. Stir until sauce is thick and slightly transparent. Serve over rice. Serves 6.

PENNSYLVANIA DUTCH POT ROAST

3 1/2 to 4-pound 7-bone beef pot roast (or similar cut such as chuck or rump roast)
1 package pot roast seasoning mix
1 medium onion, thinly sliced in rings
2 green apples, peeled and sliced about 1/2-inch thick
1/4 cup water

Place meat on a piece of aluminum foil large enough to wrap the meat. Then sprinkle with pot roast seasoning mix. Add a layer of onion rings and apples on the meat and pour water over meat. Wrap securely and place in a roasting pan. Bake in 350 degree oven for 3 hours. Makes 6 to 8 servings.

TAMALE FLANK STEAKS

2 beef flank steaks (about a pound each)
1 can (15 ounces) tamales
1/4 cup cooking oil
1 can (8 ounces) tomato sauce
1 can (10 ounces) chili hot sauce
3/4 teaspoon salt
1/8 teaspoon garlic salt
1/8 teaspoon pepper
1/4 cup strong beef broth
1 tablespoon chili powder
1 teaspoon hot sauce

Pound meat on both sides until meat is about 1/4 inch thick. Then sprinkle with salt, garlic salt and pepper. Unwrap tamales, place in bowl. Break up with fork. Spread tamales over seasoned steaks. Roll up each steak, starting with the narrow end. Tie and brown on all sides in oil. Place in shallow baking pan. Combine remaining ingredients and pour over meat. Bake at 350 degrees for 1 1/2 hours, or until tender, basting occasionally with sauce. Top each slice with sauce.

CORDON BLEU

4 lean sirloin steaks (1/3rd to 1/2 pound each)
1 teaspoon Dijon mustard
4 thin slices Danish ham
4 thin slices Svenbo or Danbo cheese
1/3 cup flour
1 teaspoon salt
1/2 teaspoon pepper
1 egg, lightly beaten
2/3 cup bread crumbs
1/3 cup butter
Lemon and parsley for garnish

Pound steaks well to about 4" x 7" size. Then spread mustard on steaks and top each steak with slice of ham and of cheese. (Both slices smaller than steaks). Fold steaks over, secure with skewers. Mix flour with spices. Dip each steak in flour on both sides, then in egg, finally in bread crumbs. Fry in butter for 4 minutes on each side until golden brown. Garnish. Serve with vegetables. Makes 4 servings.

BEEF WELLINGTON

1 4-pound eye round of beef
1/4 cup softened butter or margarine
1 teaspoon unseasoned tenderizer
1 (4-ounce) can chopped mushrooms, drained
2 (4 3/4-ounce) cans liver pate
1/4 teaspoon rosemary
2 (10-ounce) packages frozen pastry shells, thawed
1 egg
1 teaspoon milk

Spread top of eye round with softened butter or margarine. Prick with a fork at 1/2-inch intervals. Sprinkle with unseasoned tenderizer. Roast in a hot (450 degree) oven 60 minutes (medium rare), then cool completely. Meanwhile, combine chopped mushrooms, liver pate and rosemary. When beef is cool, spread liver-mushroom mixture over entire surface. Roll out 2 (10-ounce) packages thawed pastry shells (12 shells) about 1/4 inch thick making one long piece of pastry. Wrap it around the beef. Trim edges of pastry, moistening edges with water and seal by pressing together. Brush crust with egg beaten with milk. Prick crust in a few places to allow steam to escape. Roll out trimmed pastry and cut into narrow strips. Lay across dough-wrapped beef in lattice pattern. Brush these also with beaten egg and milk. Bake in hot (425 degree) oven 20 minutes, or until pastry is golden brown. Serves 8 to 10.

TERIYAKI ROUND STEAK WITH RICE

Cooked rice
1 pound round steak, trimmed and thinly sliced
2 tablespoons vegetable oil
1 onion, thinly sliced
1 garlic clove, minced
1/4 cup water
2 tablespoons soy sauce
2 tablespoons sherry or water
1 tablespoon brown sugar
1 tablespoon lemon juice
1/2 teaspoon ground ginger
1/2 teaspoon corn starch

Cook rice according to package directions. Drain and keep warm. While rice is cooking, saute steak strips in 10 inch skillet in oil, a few pieces at a time, until all are browned. Return all strips to skillet, along with the remaining ingredients, except corn starch. Mix well. Cover and simmer over moderately low heat for 20 minutes. Dissolve corn starch in small amount of water and stir into the meat mixture. Serve the teriyaki over hot steamed rice. Makes 4 servings.

SWEET AND SOUR POT ROAST

3 1/2 pounds of beef
Salt and pepper
1 quart canned tomatoes
6 medium onions (onions may be eliminated)
2 tablespoons cooking oil
1/2 cup honey
Lemon juice (optional)
2 sweet potatoes

Fry the onions, cut small, until a golden brown and set aside. Salt and pepper the meat, brown on all sides in cooking oil, cover kettle tightly and let simmer for 1 1/2 hours or until nearly tender. Add hot water only if necessary. Add fried onions, tomatoes, honey, and lemon juice if not sour enough. Finish cooking in oven until gravy is thick and meat well browned. Add 2 sweet potatoes, cut up fine, 15 or 20 minutes before meat is done.

SPICY POT ROAST

4 teaspoons salt
2 teaspoons ground mace
1 teaspoon minced garlic
1/2 teaspoon pepper
4 pounds rolled rump roast
1/2 cup apple cider vinegar
1 tablespoon salad oil
3/4 cup catsup
1/4 cup water
1 cup chopped green pepper
1 cup chopped onions

Combine first 4 ingredients, rub thoroughly into meat on all sides. Place meat in bowl and pour vinegar over meat. Cover and then marinate in refrigerator overnight, turning meat occasionally. Drain meat well. Discard marinade. Brown meat on all sides in oil in Dutch oven. Combine catsup and remaining ingredients; spoon over meat. Cover; bake in 350 degree F. oven, 2 1/2 to 3 hours or until meat is tender, basting occasionally. Skim excess fat from sauce and then, if preferred, thicken sauce. Makes 8 - 10 servings.

MEXICAN POT ROAST

4 to 5-pound pot roast, sprinkled with salt and pepper (shoulder roast is good)
1 tablespoon cooking oil
1 clove garlic chopped or put through press
1 medium onion, chopped
1 (1 pound) can peeled whole tomatoes, chopped
2 (4 ounce) cans green chilies, chopped
1/2 teaspoon oregano
1 teaspoon salt
1/2 teaspoon pepper
1/4 teaspoon crushed red pepper
2 (15 1/2 ounce) cans chili beans or red kidney beans, undrained
1 (3 1/2 ounce) can pitted ripe olives, chopped (optional)

In Dutch oven or other heavy pot heat cooking oil. Sprinkle roast with salt and pepper, then brown quickly on both sides. Remove meat temporarily. To drippings, add onion and garlic and cook over medium heat till onion is tender but not brown. Then add tomatoes, green chilies, oregano, salt, peppers and beans. Heat to boiling, then reduce heat to simmer. Return meat to Dutch oven or pot and add olives. Cover tightly; put in 350 degree oven and cook till tender (about 2 1/2 hours.) Serves 4 to 6.

BEEF MEATBALLS

1 package (8 ounces) beef flavor rice and vermicelli
1 pound ground beef
1 egg, beaten
2 1/2 cups water

Combine rice and vermicelli with ground beef and egg. Shape into small meatballs. Brown on all sides in skillet. Combine contents of flavor packet with water and pour over meatballs. Cover and simmer 30 minutes. Thicken gravy if desired. Makes 16-20 meatballs.

OLD-TIME MEAT LOAF

1 can (10 3/4 ounces) condensed cream of mushroom or golden
mushroom soup
2 pounds ground beef
1/2 cup fine dry bread crumbs
1 egg, slightly beaten
1/3 cup finely chopped onion
1 teaspoon salt
1/3 cup water

Mix thoroughly 1/2 cup soup, beef, bread crumbs, egg, onion, and
salt and then shape firmly into loaf about 4 by 8 inches. Place in
shallow baking pan and bake at 375 degrees for 75 to 80 minutes. In
saucepan, blend remaining soup, water and 2 to 3 tablespoons
drippings. Heat and stir occasionally. Serve with loaf. Makes 6 to 8
servings.

Cheese-topped Meat Loaf: Prepare loaf as above but bake for 1 hour.
Then cover loaf with 4 cups mashed potatoes and sprinkle with
shredded Cheddar cheese. Bake 15 minutes more.

CHILI MEAT LOAF

1 can (15 ounces) chili with beans
2 eggs, slightly beaten
1 medium onion, minced
1/2 cup diced green pepper
1 teaspoon salt
2 pounds lean ground beef

Pour chili into large mixing bowl. Stir in eggs and then add onion,
pepper, salt, and meat cut into pieces. Use a fork to cut through
mixture to blend it thoroughly and thereby tenderize the meat. Then
shape into loaf and place on greased shallow pan. Smooth into shape.
Bake in oven at 400 degrees for about 60 minutes. Makes 6 servings.

PEACHED SHORT RIBS

4 pounds beef short ribs
1 tablespoon vegetable oil
1 can (29 ounce) cling peach halves
1/3 cup soy sauce
1/4 cup tomato catsup
1 clove garlic, crushed

Brown ribs slowly in hot oil in Dutch oven or other heavy pot. Drain peaches but reserve 3/4 cup syrup. Mix syrup with remaining ingredients and add to ribs. Cover and then place in 350 degree oven. Bake about 2 hours, or until tender. Add peaches to ribs, return to oven 10 minutes. Makes 4 to 6 servings.

SCOTCH GLAZED HAM STEAK

1 fully-cooked ham steak, 1 inch thick
2 tablespoons brown sugar
2 teaspoons prepared mustard
1/8 teaspoon ginger
3 tablespoons Scotch

Slash outside fat of ham steak to prevent curling. Combine sugar, mustard, ginger and enough Scotch to make a paste. Warm remaining Scotch. Broil ham steak about 5 minutes until browned. Turn, broil second side about 4 minutes. Spread with brown sugar mixture and broil 1-2 minutes longer until glazed. Place ham on heated serving plate. Ignite warmed Scotch, pour flaming over ham. Serve when flames go out, spooning sauce on each portion. 2 to 3 servings.

BAKED HAM GOURMET

10-12 pound smoked ham
3/4 cup Scotch
Cloves
1 cup brown sugar
2 tablespoons dry mustard

Cook ham according to directions on package. 30 minutes before ham is done, remove rind and score fat. Cover with mixture of 1/4 cup Scotch and brown sugar and stud with cloves. Add mustard to remaining Scotch, pour over ham and continue baking, basting occasionally.

GRAVY PORK CHOPS

4 loin or rib pork chops
1 tablespoon shortening
1 12-ounce jar canned pork gravy
Salt
Pepper

In skillet over medium heat, brown 4 (3/4-inch thick) loin or rib pork chops in 1 tablespoon shortening. Drain excess fat. Season chops lightly with salt and pepper. Pour 1 jar (12 ounces) canned pork gravy over chops. Cover and let simmer 40 to 45 minutes or until pork chops are tender. Baste occasionally. Makes 4 servings.

SIMPLE PORK CHOPS

1 cup applesauce
1/4 cup soy sauce
1/8 teaspoon onion powder
6 pork chops, cut 3/4 to 1 inch thick

Brown pork chops on both sides over medium-high heat. Place in shallow baking pan side by side. Combine remaining ingredients and ladle evenly over chops. Cover pan well with foil. Place in oven at 350 degrees. Bake for about 45 minutes. Then remove foil and bake another 12-15 minutes so chops are tender.

LAMB CURRY

2 pounds boneless lamb stew meat, cut into 1-inch cubes
2 tablespoons butter or margarine
2 cups chopped onion
2 cloves garlic, minced or pressed
2 teaspoons tumeric
3/4 teaspoon salt
1/4 teaspoon each ground ginger, ground cumin, ground coriander and chili powder
1/2 cup plain yogurt
1 tablespoon all-purpose flour
1/2 cup blanched slivered almonds, toasted

Trim excess fat from lamb. In heavy skillet melt butter, saute onions and garlic until lightly browned. Remove and reserve. Then add lamb to hot skillet and cook, stirring, until well browned. Reduce heat and return onion mixture to skillet. Add tumeric, salt, ginger, cumin, coriander and chili powder. Simmer, covered, over low heat until lamb is tender, usually about an hour. (Add water if sauce becomes dry.) Stir together yogurt and flour and add to meat. Then bring to boil and stir in almonds and serve immediately. Makes 4 servings.

BUTTERFLIED LEG OF LAMB

1 leg of lamb, boned and butterflied
2 cups Claret wine
2 teaspoons poultry seasoning
2 teaspoons salt
3 cloves garlic, peeled
2 tablespoons grated onion

Place lamb, spread flat, in glass or porcelain dish. Pour over combined wine and seasonings and marinate 12 to 24 hours, turning occasionally. Grill over hot coals 20 minutes on each side; baste with marinade. Transfer to heated serving platter. Slice across grain to serve. Serves 6.

BUTTERED GRILLED CHICKEN

1 cup butter
4 fryer chickens, halved
1 tablespoon salt
1/2 teaspoon black pepper
1/2 teaspoon cayenne pepper
2 teaspoons poultry seasoning

Melt butter in small pan and stir in salt, pepper, and poultry seasoning. Place chicken in shallow dish and then pour marinade over chicken. Cover and marinade 3 hours in refrigerator.

Place aluminum foil on grate 3-10 inches from charcoal. Place chicken halves, skin side up, on aluminum foil. Brush with marinade. Close aluminum foil tightly. Cook until brown and tender, turning and brushing occasionally. Grill 1 to 1 1/4 hours. Aluminum foil may be removed last 15 minutes for crisp chicken.

BARBECUED CHICKEN

1 chicken
1 cup celery--chopped
2 onions
1/2 cup green pepper
2 tablespoons brown sugar
1 can stewed tomatoes (2 cups)
2 tablespoons vinegar
1/2 teaspoon prepared mustard
1 1/2 tablespoons worcestershire sauce
1 cup tomato sauce
1 cup mushrooms
1 teaspoon salt

Salt chicken lightly. Roll the chicken in flour, place in skillet and brown. Fry the onions, mushrooms, green pepper and celery until the onions are a golden brown in 1/2 cup butter. Add sugar, salt, tomatoes, vinegar, mustard, worcestershire sauce, tomato sauce and cook 5 minutes. Then pour over chicken and bake for 30 minutes at 375 degrees.

HONEY MUSTARD CHICKEN

1/2 cup salad dressing
2 tablespoons mustard (use Dijon for added zest)
1 tablespoon honey
4 boneless skinless chicken breast halves (about 1 1/4 pounds)

Mix salad dressing, mustard and honey. Place chicken on greased grill over medium-hot coals (coals will have slight glow) or rack of broiler pan 5 to 7 inches from heat. Brush with 1/2 of the salad dressing mixture. Grill or broil 8 to 10 minutes. Turn; brush with remaining salad dressing mixture. Continue grilling or broiling 8 to 10 minutes or until tender. Serves 4.

FRIED CHICKEN

1 chicken, cut in serving pieces
3/4 cup flour
1 teaspoon salt
1/4 teaspoon pepper
1/2 - 1 teaspoon paprika
Cooking oil

Put flour, salt, pepper and paprika in a medium-sized paper sack and shake to mix. Add chicken, a few pieces at a time, and shake to coat with flour mixture. Heat oil in frying pan on medium heat. Then add chicken and cook until chicken is done. Or brown well and remove to pan and finish cooking in oven. (Cooking time in both cases is 45 minutes to 1 hour.) Add flour to pan drippings, stir and add milk, salt and pepper to make gravy.

ORANGE GLAZED CHICKEN

4 chicken breasts
1/3 cup butter or margarine, melted
1 1/2 teaspoon salt
1/2 teaspoon pepper
1 5 ounce can frozen orange juice concentrate
1/2 teaspoon ginger

Wash chicken breasts and dab dry with a paper towel. Melt butter in saucepan. Then, using a pastry brush, coat chicken on both sides with butter. Combine salt and pepper and sprinkle over each breast. Place chicken, skin-side up, in shallow baking pan. Bake at 350 degrees for 30 minutes, basting occasionally with melted butter. Combine orange juice with remaining butter in saucepan and add ginger. Heat until juice is melted. Then thoroughly coat both sides of chicken with orange glaze. Bake for 20 minutes longer.

SOUTHWEST-STYLE CHICKEN WINGS

12 chicken wings
1 cup picante sauce
1/3 cup catsup
1/4 cup honey
1/4 teaspoon ground cumin
2/3 cup sour cream

Cut wings in half at joints and discard tips. Combine 1/3 cup picante sauce, catsup, honey and cumin and pour over chicken. Refrigerate at least 1 hour, turning once. Drain chicken, reserving marinade. Place on rack of foil-lined broiler pan. Bake at 375 degrees, 30 minutes. Brush with marinade; turn and bake, brushing with marinade every 10 minutes, until tender (usually about 30 minutes). Place 6 inches from heat in broiler and broil 2 minutes or until sauce looks dry. Turn and broil 2 minutes again, or until sauce looks dry. Place sour cream in small bowl; top with remaining picante sauce. Serve with chicken. Makes 24 appetizers.

KENTUCKY CHICKEN

2 cups bread crumbs
3/4 cup Parmesan cheese
1/4 cup fresh parsley leaves
2 teaspoons salt
1/8 teaspoon pepper
1 clove garlic, crushed
3 pounds chicken breasts
1 cup melted butter

Mix bread crumbs with cheese, parsley, salt, pepper and garlic. Dip each piece of chicken into melted butter, then into crumb mixture. Coat well. Arrange in shallow roasting pan. Pour remaining butter over all. Bake at 350 degrees for 1 hour or until tender. Do not turn chicken; baste frequently with pan drippings. Serves 8-10.

HOW TO MAKE SALAMI

2 pounds hamburger
1/8 teaspoon powdered garlic
1/2 teaspoon coarse pepper
3 tablespoons Morton Tender Quick Salt
1 cup water
1/4 teaspoon mustard seed

Mix well and then shape into 2 or 3 small rolls. Wrap in foil, fasten ends with twists and place in refrigerator for 24 hours. Then put in a large saucepan and cover with water. Bring to a boil and boil for 1 hour. Using a fork, stab a few holes in bottom of foil and refrigerate.

TURKEY VEGETABLE PIE

1 package frozen peas
1 package frozen mixed vegetables
2 tablespoons fat
1 onion, diced
2 cups cooked, cubed turkey
1 1/2 tablespoons flour
1 1/2 cups mixed broth and milk
Salt
Pepper
1 recipe biscuits

Cook vegetables as directed on packages and then drain. Melt fat and add onion and simmer until tender. Add meat to skillet and cook for a few minutes, stirring constantly. Remove meat mixture from skillet. Add flour and broth and cook until well blended. Mix meat mixture, vegetables and sauce. Season to taste. Pour into greased dish. Cover with thinly rolled biscuits. Bake at 425 degrees for 30 minutes. Serves 6.

TURKEY WITH BROCCOLI

1 small turkey breast (1 pound), cut in thin strips
1/2 cup water
1 tablespoon cornstarch
2 tablespoons soy sauce
1/4 teaspoon ginger
6 tablespoons vegetable oil
1/2 pound mushrooms, sliced
1 head of broccoli (1/2 pound); stems cut in 1/4-inch slices,
Florets in bite-size pieces
1 teaspoon salt

In a small bowl, combine 1/4 cup of water, cornstarch, soy sauce, and ginger. Set aside. In a wok or skillet, heat 4 tablespoons of oil. Add turkey and stir-fry 1 minute. Add mushrooms and stir-fry 30 seconds. Remove turkey and mushrooms from pan and set aside. Add remaining 2 tablespoons of oil, broccoli stems, and salt. Stir-fry 30 seconds. Add broccoli florets and stir-fry 1 minute. Add remaining 1/4 cup of water; cover and cook over medium heat 3 minutes. Return turkey and mushrooms to pan; stir-fry on high heat for 1 minute. Push turkey and vegetables up side of wok or skillet; gradually stir cornstarch mixture into boiling liquid. Cook until thick and clear, stirring constantly. Mix meat and vegetables into sauce. Serve with rice.

GRILLED LEMON/HONEY CHICKEN

6 1 1/2 to 2 pound broiler-fryers, split
2 cups salad oil
1/2 cup lime or lemon juice
2 teaspoons salt
1/4 cup honey

Wash chicken halves and then dry. Mix salad oil, juice and salt in saucepan. Brush over chickens. Place chickens, skin-side up, on grill about six inches above hot coals. Grill for 1 hour, turning and brushing often with sauce. Stir honey into remaining sauce; brush over chickens. Continue grilling for 15 minutes or until brown and done, brushing often with sauce.

GRILLED SEAFOOD STEAKS

2 pounds fish steaks, fresh or frozen
1/2 cup oil
1/4 cup lemon juice
2 teaspoons salt
1/2 teaspoon Worcestershire sauce
1/4 teaspoon white pepper
Dash liquid hot pepper sauce
Paprika

Cut steaks to desired serving size and place on greased grill. Combine remaining ingredients, except paprika. Baste with sauce and sprinkle with paprika. Cook about 5 to 6 inches from moderate hot coals for 8 to 10 minutes. Baste and sprinkle with paprika, turn and cook for 7-10 minutes longer until fish flakes easily when tested with a fork. Serves 6.

TUNA BUNS

1 can tuna fish
2 - 3 hard boiled eggs, grated
1/4 - 1/2 cup grated cheese
1 celery stick chopped
Salad dressing as needed
Buns

Mix above items, fill buns. Wrap in foil, heat in oven.

FRIED TROUT

4 or 5 small trout
3/4 cup flour, seasoned with salt, pepper and pinch of thyme
6 tablespoons cooking oil
1/2 cup butter
3 tablespoons lemon juice
4 tablespoons parsley, chopped
1 tablespoon chopped chives
8 lemon slices, dipped in paprika
1/2 cup chopped mushrooms

Roll trout in seasoned flour. Heat oil in fry pan and set trout in carefully. Cook thoroughly until well browned on both sides. While fish is cooking, brown butter in sauce pan, add chopped mushrooms and saute for about 5 minutes. Add lemon juice, chopped parsley, chives and dash of salt. Heat thoroughly and pour over trout. Serve while warm. Add a slice of lemon for added flavor as desired.

BAKED SALMON

4 1-pound fish or 1 4-pound fish
2 tablespoons melted margarine
1/2 cup chopped parsley
1/4 cup chopped dill sprigs or 3 whole dill seeds
1/4 cup chopped chives
1/4 cup chopped onion
2 tablespoons lemon juice

Rinse and drain fish. Mix above ingredients and pack inside fish. Wrap in foil, letting no air escape. Bake at 400 degrees for 20 to 25 minutes. Best served warm.

PAN FRIED FISH

1 tablespoon shortening or oil
3 pounds fillets
1 egg, slightly beaten
3 tablespoons milk
1/2 cup corn meal
1/2 cup flour
1 teaspoon salt
1/8 teaspoon pepper

Heat shortening in frying pan over moderate heat. Cut fish in serving pieces. Dip in mixture of egg and milk and then shake in bag containing the corn meal and flour. Place fish in pan and leave over medium heat for 3 to 4 minutes; cover, reduce heat and cook 3 more minutes. Remove cover, sprinkle with salt and pepper, turn, and cook on second side an additional 3 to 4 minutes, raising the heat a bit and sprinkling with salt and pepper. Provide a wedge of lemon with each serving to add a bit of zest. Note: This recipe also works wonderfully for pan frying small brook trout. Serves 6.

FISH FILLETS

2 pounds fresh or frozen fish fillets
2 egg whites
1/2 cup mayonnaise
1 teaspoon prepared mustard
1/2 teaspoon salt
1/8 teaspoon pepper

Place fillets in a lightly greased baking dish. Beat egg whites until stiff. Fold in mixture of mayonnaise, mustard, salt and pepper. Spread on fillets. Bake at 400 degrees for 15-20 minutes or until fish is flaky and topping is brown. Serves 6.

BAKED OR BARBECUED SALMON
An All-Purpose Recipe

Wipe whole or half salmon with damp paper towel. Salt inside cavity and fill with slices of lemon and onion, if desired. Brush skin with salad oil or French Dressing. Place salmon in a spit basket or on a flip grill and rotisserate or barbecue over slow coals. If you prefer to bake, place on rack in baking pan and bake at 350 degrees for 12 to 15 minutes per pound or until done. For a slightly different, zesty taste, barbecue with a marinade or sauce of lemon juice and oil or a commercial French Dressing.

BARBECUED OYSTERS

Place unshelled oysters (or clams) on top of the barbecue grill with the short hinge up. Allow oysters to steam and barbecue in their own juice. When the oysters open, do not drain the juice, but let the oysters cook a few more minutes. This solidifes the meat. Then unhinge the top of the shell and serve on the half shell with a bit of lemon juice or possibly a bit of paprika.

TERIYAKI SAUCE

1/2 cup soy sauce
4 tablespoons sugar
2 tablespoons corn syrup
1/2 cup soft butter or margarine or salad oil

Brush on fish several times during cooking.

BARBECUED SALMON

1 whole salmon, dressed (allow about 1/2 pound per person)
1 recipe Teriyaki sauce (opposite page)
1 medium onion, quartered

Marinate salmon in Teriyaki Sauce for at least 6 hours or overnight. Place onion in cavity of salmon and secure with skewers. Place salmon in a spit basket or on a flip grill and barbecue over slow coals. Baste frequently with Teriyaki sauce while barbecuing. Toss wet hickory chips or green leaves over coals for a delicate smoke flavor. Allow 60 to 80 minutes for a medium-sized fish and up to two hours for a larger one.

BARBECUED HALIBUT

3 to 4 pound halibut
1 can tomato sauce or 1 cup catsup
2 tablespoons chopped onion
1 tablespoon salad oil
2 tablespoons vinegar
1/4 cup lemon juice
3 tablespoons Worcestershire sauce
2 tablespoons brown sugar
1/2 teaspoon salt
Dash of pepper

Mix all ingredients except fish in saucepan and bring to boiling point. Simmer for 6 minutes. Brush both sides of fish with sauce. Then wrap in foil to catch drippings but leave open at top. Place on outdoor barbecue grill or under oven broiler. Fish is done when it flakes easily.

BAKED TROUT

1 large trout
1 cup dry white wine
1 cup bread crumbs
Saute in:
6 tablespoons butter
3/4 cup chopped onion
1/2 cup chopped parsley

Put 1/3 of this mixture at the bottom of a well buttered shallow baking pan. Place fish on this and fill cavity, which has been well salted and peppered, with another 1/3 of the sauted mixture. Place last 1/3 of mixture on top of fish. Add 1 cup of dry white wine to pan. Cover and bake at 350 degrees until done. Test with fork. Uncover, sprinkle with 1 cup bread crumbs and just before serving place under broiler until crumbs are brown. Remove and garnish. This fish is also excellent stuffed with a dry bread stuffing with onion, parsley and butter added.

SWEET MUSTARD-SAUCED FISH

1 1/2 pounds fresh or frozen fish fillets
1/2 cup salsa
2 tablespoons mayonnaise or salad dressing
2 tablespoons honey
2 tablespoons prepared mustard

Cut fish into 6 portions. Place in a 13x9x2-inch baking dish. Bake, uncovered, in a 450 degree oven for 4 to 6 minutes per 1/2-inch thickness or till fish just flakes easily with a fork. Drain off any liquid. Meanwhile, stir together salsa, mayonnaise, honey, and mustard; spoon over drained fish. Return to oven for 2 to 3 minutes or till sauce is heated through. Transfer to individual dinner plates; spoon sauce remaining in dish over fish. Makes 6 servings.

HALIBUT A LA GRECO

1 1/2 pounds fresh or frozen halibut steaks, 3/4 inch thick
2 tablespoons margarine or butter
1 beaten egg
1/3 cup light cream or milk
1 cup crumbled feta cheese
1/8 teaspoon ground red pepper
1 large tomato, chopped (1 cup)
1/4 cup chopped pitted ripe olives
1/4 cup toasted pine nuts or slivered almonds
1 tablespoon lemon juice
1 tablespoon snipped parsley
1/8 teaspoon pepper

Cut halibut into 6 portions. In a large skillet cook halibut in margarine or butter over medium-high heat for 3 minutes on each side. (Halibut will be partially cooked.) Transfer to a 12x7 1/2 x 2-inch baking dish. In a small bowl stir together egg and cream or milk. Stir in cheese and red pepper; spoon over halibut. Sprinkle with tomato, olives and nuts. Bake, uncovered, in a 400 degree oven for 10 minutes or till fish just flakes when tested with a fork. Sprinkle with lemon juice, parsley, and pepper. Makes 6 servings.

BARBECUED TROUT

1 4-5 pound trout

Clean and scale. Wash thoroughly. Salt and pepper. Rub the inside of fish with lemon juice. Baste fish with butter and lemon juice; then top with slices of lemon. Wrap in aluminum foil and place on barbecue until done — 1 hour to 1 1/2 hours depending on size of fish.

SNAPPER

2 pounds red snapper steaks or fillets
1/2 teaspoon salt
1/4 teaspoon pepper
1 can (4 ounces) mushrooms, drained
1/2 cup chopped green onions
1/4 cup catsup
2 tablespoons melted butter or margarine
1/2 teaspoon liquid smoke (optional)

Cut snapper into serving size portions. Place in greased baking dish. Sprinkle with salt and pepper. Combine remaining ingredients and spread over fish. Bake in 350 degree oven for 20 to 25 minutes or until flaky. Serves 6.

FRIED TROUT

Trout
Cornmeal
Salt
Pepper
Bacon grease
Egg
Crackers

Roll trout in mixture of cornmeal, salt and pepper. Fry in bacon grease (or oil) until done. Can also dip in beaten egg and roll in cracker crumbs seasoned with season salt.

WILD GAME
&
BISON

VENISON SWISS STEAK

3/4 cup flour
2 teaspoons salt
1/4 teaspoon pepper
4 venison steaks
3 tablespoons fat
2 tablespoons onion salt

Combine flour, salt and pepper. Cut steak into smaller servings and then pound dry ingredients into steak. Brown in hot fat in Dutch oven or other heavy pot. Sprinkle each piece with onion salt. Remove meat and make gravy. Then place meat back in pot and cover. Cook over low heat for 90 minutes or until steak is tender. Serves 6.

WILD MEAT & SAUCE

1 to 1 1/2 pounds deer or antelope meat, cut into 1-inch squares
1/4 cup flour
3 to 4 tablespoons cooking oil
1/8 teaspoon garlic
1/4 teaspoon oregano
Salt and pepper to taste
1 8 ounce can tomato sauce (optional)
Water

Dredge meat in flour and then brown well in hot oil. Add remaining flour and seasonings; brown slightly. Add tomato sauce and enough water to make thin sauce. Then cook for 90 minutes over very low heat until oil separates, adding liquid as needed. Note: Deer or elk meat may replace antelope. Serves 4.

ROAST VENISON

2 pound venison roast
2 cups vinegar
4 cups water
Salt and pepper to taste
1/2 cup flour
1/4 cup cooking oil

Place roast in glass container and pour vinegar over roast. Refrigerate for 24 hours. Drain vinegar and then soak roast in same container in 2 cups water for 10 to 12 hours. Drain water and dry roast before seasoning with salt and pepper. Sprinkle one-half flour on roast. Melt fat in 8-inch roaster. Sear roast to medium brown on all sides and then remove from roaster. Add remaining flour, 1/2 teaspoonful salt and 1/2 teaspoonful pepper to fat and brown. Reduce heat, add remaining water, and place roast in pan. Cover and cook for 90 minutes. Serves 6.

PAT'S HAMBURGERS AND TOMATO SAUCE

2 pounds hamburger
1 package dry onion soup
2 eggs
1 large can tomato soup

Mix hamburger with package of dry onion soup and 2 eggs. Form into patties and fry on hot griddle or frypan until almost done. Pour 1 large can tomato soup over the patties and simmer for 10 minutes. This is one of Dunc's favorites. Serves 6.

Courtesy Pat Gilchrist, Hamilton, Montana

SLOPPY JOES

1 1/2 to 2 pounds ground venison
1 tablespoon oil
1 medium onion (diced) or 2 tablespoons minced dry onion
2 8 ounce cans tomato sauce
1 teaspoon dry mustard
1 1/2 to 2 teaspoons chili powder
1 1/2 teaspoons sugar
1/2 teaspoon Tabasco sauce
2 tablespoons vinegar
1/2 to 1/4 cup water
1 package hamburger buns

Set buns aside. Brown meat in oil in skillet. Add onion and cook
slightly. Then add remaining ingredients. Stir to blend and then
cover and simmer for 60 to 90 minutes, stirring occasionally. Add
more water if needed. Serve on warm, buttered buns. Note: Ground
elk or antelope work well too. Serves 4 to 6.

POT ROAST

Melted bacon fat or shortening
1 venison pot roast
1/2 cup dry red wine or 2 oranges and rind
1 bay leaf
6 peppercorns
2 carrots, halved
2 celery stalks with tops
1 orange
1 onion, halved
3 tablespoons flour
Seasoning to taste
2 tablespoons thick sour cream

Grease Dutch oven with tight fitting lid or a medium-sized pot with a small amount of bacon fat. Brown roast well on all sides. Add 1 cup water, wine, bay leaf, peppercorns, carrots and celery. Squeeze orange over meat and then set rind on meat. Add onion. Cover tightly. Bake at 350 degrees for 2 hours or until done. Remove roast from oven but keep hot. Strain liquid and skim off fat. Then add enough bacon fat to skimmed fat to make 1/3 cup. Return fat to Dutch oven and blend in flour. Use low heat on top of stove and then blend in remaining pan liquid and a small amount of water, as needed. Stir until it thickens. Add seasonings and stir in sour cream. Serves 6.

VENISON BACON RECIPE

Use fully trimmed loin or portion of lean roast (no fat), from deer, elk, moose, antelope or beef. Divide meat in half for easier handling, using from one to one and one-half pound pieces.

Ingredients (to season 3 pounds of meat):
2 teaspoons Mortons Tender Quick Salt per pound of meat
1/2 cup cornmeal
1/4 teaspoon course ground black pepper
1/4 teaspoon chili powder
1/4 teaspoon season-all
1/4 teaspoon sage

Place loin on clean surface and rub in Tender Quick. When all salt is absorbed, place in double plastic bag and place in refrigerator for six days, turning over daily.

Then mix together cornmeal, pepper, chili powder, sage, and season-all. Remove meat from plastic bag and place on clean surface. Cover the meat with this mixture, rubbing and rolling until entire surface area is coated. Place in clean plastic bag and return to refrigerator for twelve hours. Slice 1/4 inch thick and fry as Canadian Bacon.

I've used this recipe for years, I hope you enjoy it.
Courtesy W. Lon Hoppe

WILD GAME SWISS STEAK

(Equally delicious with moose, elk, venison or antelope.)

2 pounds round or sirloin steak
Salt and pepper
Flour
Oil
1 onion
1 clove garlic, finely chopped (optional)
1/4 cup green pepper, chopped
1/4 cup celery, chopped
1 can (8 ounces) canned tomatoes

Cut steak into serving size pieces. Salt and pepper meat. Pound about 3/4 cup flour into steak with meat mallet or handle of a table knife. Brown well on both sides and add chopped onions, garlic, green pepper and celery. Cook slightly. Add tomatoes, cover and cook over low heat for about 2 hours. May also be transferred to 325 degree oven to finish cooking.

HOT VENISON SANDWICHES

1 4-pound venison roast
1 small onion, diced
1/2 pint tomato juice
1 can tomato sauce
Salt to taste
1/2 teaspoon pepper
2 teaspoons Worcestershire sauce
1/2 teaspoon garlic salt
1 teaspoon hot sauce (optional)
4 hamburger buns, split

Place roast in roasting pan. Add onion, tomato juice, tomato sauce, salt and pepper. Cover and bake at 400 degrees for 2 hours. Remove roast from pan. Cool. Add Worcestershire sauce, garlic salt and hot sauce to pan drippings; stir well. Slice meat and place in drippings for savoring. Heat just before serving and spoon juices and meat over buns. Serves 6 to 8.

VENISON POT PIE

2 pounds tender venison meat cut into 1 inch cubes
4 tablespoons flour
2 teaspoons salt
Pepper to taste
1/2 cup cooking oil
1/2 teaspoon garlic powder
3 1/2 cups water
2 beef bouillon cubes
1/4 cup sliced carrots
1/2 cup chopped celery
1/2 cup onion
2 cups fresh or frozen peas
Biscuit dough
Melted butter

Dredge meat with flour, salt and pepper. Brown slowly and add any remaining flour. Reduce heat. Add 1 cup water with bouillon cubes. Then cover and simmer 1 1/2 hours or until meat is tender. Add remaining water as needed. Add the vegetables and simmer another 1/2 hour. Pour hot stew mixture into a large dutch oven. Top with biscuit dough rolled to 1/2 inch thickness, flute edges and brush with butter. Cut vents in center. (Or drop by spoonfuls to make individual biscuits.) Bake in hot 450 degree oven for 12 to 15 minutes until crust is brown. Serve while hot.

ROLLED VENISON
(ANTELOPE, ELK, DEER)

1 venison round steak (remove bone, trim fat & pound)
1/4 pound bacon (cut in half)
1 teaspoon salt
1/2 teaspoon garlic powder
Dash of pepper
1/2 cup onion (chopped fine)
1/2 cup flour
1 teaspoon paprika
1 can cream of mushroom soup
4 tablespoon butter

Cut pounded steak into medium size squares, then sprinkle with salt, garlic powder and pepper. Place chopped onion and bacon strips on steak and roll up (like a jelly roll) and fasten with tooth picks or tie with string. Roll steak rolls in flour, brown rolls in butter. Pour soup over steak rolls, simmer in covered pot for 1 hour or until tender.

Courtesy Sonny Templeton, Lincoln, Montana

POT ROAST

1 package dry onion soup mix
1 4-pound venison roast

Sprinkle one-half package soup mix on large sheet of aluminum foil. Place roast on soup mix and then sprinkle remaining soup mix over meat. Wrap tightly. Place in shallow pan and roast at 450 degrees for 1 hour. Reduce heat to 350 degrees and roast for 2 hours and 30 minutes. Note: If soup mix is not availble, use 1 cup sliced celery, 1 cup celery leaves and 1/2 teaspoonful garlic powder or garlic salt.

NOODLES & VENISON

1 pound ground venison
3 tablespoons shortening
1/2 cup chopped onion
1 cup diced celery
1/2 cup chopped green pepper
1 small can kidney beans
1 quart tomatoes
2 cups broad noodles, uncooked
1 small can mushrooms (optional)
1 teaspoon salt
1/8 teaspoon pepper

Brown meat in lightly greased large skillet. Add onion, celery and green pepper and then saute until vegetables are transparent. Add remaining ingredients and mix well. Cover and bring to a boil. Then reduce heat and let simmer for 20 minutes. Serves 6.

BARBECUED VENISON

2 chopped onions
6 tablespoons salad or canola oil
2 tablespoons sugar
2 teaspoons dry mustard
2 teaspoons paprika
1 cup water
1/2 cup vinegar
2 tablespoons Worcestershire sauce
2 drops of Tabasco sauce (optional)
Sliced cooked venison

Brown onions in salad oil. Add remaining ingredients except venison. Arrange meat in casserole. Pour sauce over meat and bake at 375 degrees until sauce thickens, usually about 20 minutes.

TERIYAKI

My favorite taste treat is cubes of choice big game soaked in teriyaki sauce. The result is broiled on a stick over an open fire. Any wild or domestic meat can be used. After traveling around the game fields of the world I have found that my favorite meats prepared in this fashion are from Dall sheep and New Zealand tahr. I use a choice cut like the tenderloin or backstrap and cut it into approximately one inch cubes. The sauce can be bought as either a liquid, or a powder. When backpacking I use the powder, otherwise the liquid is just fine. The meat should be soaked for a minimum of a half hour before cooking. We generally heat the remaining sauce for dipping the cooked meat. At home we often cook our meat on skewers, under a broiler.

A real London Broil is made from a beef tenderloin, but we use a much smaller backstrap from a big game animal. Soaking in teriyaki before cooking is optional, and we generally do. Wrap strips of bacon around the meat, to help replace the lack of natural fats, and broil until done. We like ours medium rare. When done slice thin and serve with a side dish of fried mushrooms and onions. People who claim they don't like wild meat generally eat this treat with gusto.

Courtesy Duncan Gilchrist, Hamilton, Montana

WILD GAME IN MUSHROOM GRAVY

Venison or quail
3 tablespoons flour
1 teaspoon salt
1/8 teaspoon pepper
3 tablespoons fat
1 can cream of mushroom soup
1/2 soup can of water

Clean meat thoroughly with water and then dry. Cut into small portions and roll meat in flour, salt and pepper. Brown meat well in hot fat. Remove from pan, place into deep baking dish. Add soup and water to pan drippings and blend well. Then pour this gravy over meat. Cover and bake at 350 degrees for 90 minutes. Note: pheasant, venison steak, quail, grouse or partridge may be used in this recipe. Serves 6.

VENISON JERKY

3 pounds fresh venison
Liquid smoke

Salt mixture:
3 tablespoons salt
1 teaspoon brown sugar
1/2 teaspoon garlic salt
1 teaspoon seasoning salt
Pepper coarsely ground

This is a recipe for jerky that you can easily make in an oven. Any piece of venison can be used, but while this is an excellent way to use the less desired cuts or those that you'd generally make into stew or hamburger, you also can make excellent jerky out of potential steak or roast meat. For easiest handling, slightly freeze the meat and then slice it into thin strips across the grain. Then spread the salt mixture on one side of the meat, brush the other side with a little bit of the liquid smoke. Stack the meat in layers in a flat pan, alternating the smoky side against the salted side. Cover with another pan, weight it down and set overnight so meat juice is pressed out. The next day, drain off juice and then grind fresh pepper over the meat. Then line bottom of oven with foil to catch drips, place the pan on oven rack at about 250 to 275 degrees and leave the meat for 5 to 6 hours, or until dry. Sometimes it takes a bit longer. Store in closed containers and store where cool.

GRILLED ELK STEAK

Elk steaks
Salt and pepper
Garlic powder

Sprinkle steaks with salt, pepper and garlic powder. Place on a grill and cook over campfire coals or on gas or charcoal barbecue. Add your favorite barbecue chips directly on campfire coals or charcoal barbecues — a few at a time, or in an aluminum pan under the grill on a gas barbecue to smolder and enhance the flavor of grilled meat. Turn and cook both sides. Cook as desired. Moose, thickly-cut deer steaks, as well as beef, are all superb when prepared this way.

WILD GAME HAMBURGER

Most people age wild meat, but if it is to be made into burger, the process is entirely unnecessary, and undesirable. Aging tenderizes meat and so does the grinding of hamburger. Almost as a matter of habit, people add beef suet to their burger. Beef fat (suet) will turn rancid in time and imparts a bad taste. Pork fat doesn't have the undesirable qualities of suet, plus it helps hold the meat together better. For the best in game burgers add 30% pork trimmings.

Courtesy Duncan Gilchrist, Hamilton, Montana

MOOSE ROAST

Salt and pepper
Garlic
Onion salt
Moose roast
1 can cream of mushroom soup
Celery (optional)
Parsley (optional)

Sprinkle salt, pepper, garlic and onion salt in greased, foil-lined pan. Place roast in foil. Pour soup over roast and season again. Close foil tight, but leave a spot open for steam to escape. Bake at 200 degrees for 1 hour per pound. Let stand for 1 hour before opening.

SWEET AND SOUR VENISON SPARERIBS

3 pounds venison spareribs
2 1/2 cups water
4 tablespoons soy sauce
Salt to taste
3 tablespoons vinegar
3 tablespoons sugar
2 tablespoons cornstarch

Cut ribs crosswise into short pieces. Place ribs, 2 cups water, soy sauce and salt in saucepan and bring to boil. Then let simmer for 1 hour. Remove ribs and place in skillet. Mix vinegar, sugar, cornstarch and remaining water and add to liquid from ribs, stirring well. Cook until mixture is thickened and clear and then pour over ribs in skillet. Cook until meat is tender. Serves 6.

VENISON CASSEROLE

1 pound ground venison
1 large onion, chopped
1 Number 2 can green beans, drained
1/2 pound noodles, cooked
1 can cream of mushroom soup
1 can tomato soup
1/4 cup grated cheese

Saute meat with onion in small amount of fat. Place in casserole and then layer in beans, noodles and soups. Sprinkle with cheese. Bake at 350 degrees for 45 minutes. Serves 6.

WILD GAME SAUSAGES

Sausage can be made from deer, elk, antelope, moose and other wild meat that has been trimmed of fat. Lean meat from any part of the carcass can be used for sausage. Please consider these points:

• Beef, pork or lamb meat can be substituted for the game, but if it contains fat, a corresponding reduction in the amount of added fat must be made.

• Speed in sausage preparation is necessary to prevent bacterial growth. Meat should be removed from the carcass, cleaned and trimmed of fat, chilled at 30 degrees and then either made into sausage the day after the kill or immediately frozen for later thawing and preparation.

• Casings that have been preserved in dry salt must be soaked in lukewarm water before use. They are then flushed by putting the end of a casing over the cold water tap and running cold water through it.

• Casings that come in a brine should also be soaked in cold water before use.

• Some artificial casings should be soaked in hot tap water for at least 30 minutes but not more than four hours before use. They should be punctured with a knife point before sausage is stuffed unless the casings come pre-punctured.

• The cure called for in some recipes contains 6.25 percent sodium nitrite, which gives a red, cured color to the sausage after it is heated. Complete cures often are available at grocery stores or locker plants. If a complete cure is used, follow the directions that come with it, for the complete cure will often replace most of the salt and sugar called for in the sausages recipes that follow.

• The following recipes call for pork or beef fat. The pork fat is preferable, but beef fat usually is easier to purchase.

• The recipes, which make 25-pound batches, can be halved.

• A meat thermometer must be used to check the internal temperature of cooked sausages such as Thuringer and cooked salami. The temperatures specified in the following recipes are all in Fahrenheit.

- *Fresh sausage must be thoroughly cooked before eating.*
- *Fresh sausage has a refrigerator shelf life of four to five days, while fresh or cooked sausage can be kept for two to three months at 0 degrees.*

COOKED SALAMI

19 pounds lean game meat
6 pounds pork or beef fat
1 cup salt
1/2 cup sugar
1 quart cold water
5 1/4 cups nonfat dry milk
6 tablespoons ground black pepper
3 tablespoons garlic powder
3 tablespoons coriander seed
4 teaspoons ground mace
4 tablespoons ground cardamom
2 tablespoons cure

Cut the meat and fat into 1-inch squares or grind through a coarse (1/2 to 1-inch) plate. Season by sprinkling remaining ingredients over the meat and hand mix. Grind through a 1/8-inch plate. Mix for 6 minutes and then stuff into natural or artificial casings 2 to 3 inches in diameter.Place in smokehouse and heat at 185 degrees until the internal sausage temperature reaches 152 degrees. Move to a cold water bath and keep it there until the internal temperature of the sausage is 100 degrees. Rinse briefly with hot water to remove grease and then hang sausage at room temperature for 2 to 3 hours before refrigeration. The salami should be cooled overnight in a refrigerator before cutting.

Salami can be roasted in casings in a 185-degree oven if a smokehouse is not available. If desired, 1 to 2 ounces of liquid smoke can be added for flavor. The sausage should then be chilled according to directions in the previous paragraph.

FRESH GAME SAUSAGE

15 pounds lean game meat
10 pounds pork or beef fat
3/4 cup salt
6 tablespoons ground black pepper
5 tablespoons rubbed sage

Cut lean meat and fat into 1-inch squares or grind through a coarse (1/2 to 1-inch) plate. Season by sprinkling the ingredients over the meat and hand mix. Then grind through a 3/16-inch plate.

Sausage can be frozen in packages, made into patties or stuffed into hog casings.

This recipe makes a mild sausage. For a more highly seasoned sausage, increase the amount of pepper and add additional seasoning such as 1 tablespoon each of nutmeg, ginger and mace.

FRESH THURINGER

20 pounds lean game meat
5 pounds pork or beef fat
4 tablespoons sugar
1 quart cold water
3/4 cup salt
3/4 cup ground white pepper
5 teaspoons powdered mustard
2 tablespoons cure
1 ounce liquid smoke (optional)

Cut lean meat and fat into 1-inch squares or grind through a coarse (1/2 to 1-inch) plate. Season by sprinkling the dry ingredients over the meat and hand mix. Grind through a 1/4-inch plate while adding water and then regrind through a 1/8-inch plate. Mix 6 minutes and then stuff into hog casings and link.

Cook Thuringer in 170-degree water or in a 185-degree smokehouse until the internal sausage temperature is 152 degrees. Then chill in cold water until sausage has an internal temperature of 100 degrees. Allow Thuringer to stand at room temperature for 1 to 2 hours and then place in refrigerator or freezer.

LIVER SAUSAGE

9 pounds liver
5 pounds lean game meat
4 pounds pork or beef fat
1 pound fresh onions
3 1/2 cups plus 2 tablespoons nonfat dry milk
4 tablespoons ground white pepper
7 tablespoons salt
4 tablespoons cure (optional)

Fry the liver until it is about half-cooked. Grind the liver, lean meat and fat through a coarse (1/2 to 1-inch) plate. Chop the onions and sprinkle them and the remaining ingredients over the meat. Hand mix. Grind through a 1/8-inch plate. Mix for 6 minutes and then stuff into natural or artificial casings 2 to 3 inches in diameter. Cook in water at 170 degrees or in a 185-degree smokehouse until internal temperature of the sausage reaches 152 degrees. Immediately place the sausage in cold water and keep it there until the internal temperature of the sausage is 100 degrees. Rinse briefly with hot water to remove grease. Allow to dry 1 to 2 hours at room temperature and then refrigerate.

SWEET AND SOUR BEAR OVER RICE

2-3 pounds bear meat
Salt and pepper
Flour
Shortening
1/2 cup water
1/4 cup wine vinegar
2 tablespoons soy sauce.
1 cup apricot or peach jam
1 small can crushed pineapple
1 green pepper, diced
1 small onion, diced

Cut meat into 1 inch cubes. Salt and pepper and coat with flour. Brown in shortening. Add water, vinegar and soy sauce. Cover and simmer for 1 hour. Add jam, pineapple, green pepper and onion and cook 20-30 minutes more. Serve over hot rice.
Note: This is also delicious made with pork meat.
Courtesy Duncan Gilchrist, Hamilton, Montana

BEAR ROAST

1 4-5 pound bear roast
Vinegar
Bacon grease or oil
1/2 teaspoon poultry seasoning
1/2 teaspoon savory salt
1/2 teaspoon garlic powder
1/2 teaspoon salt

Wipe roast with vinegar soaked cloth and dry. Lightly coat with grease or oil. Mix spices and rub into roast. Place meat in roaster with about 1 inch of water. Cover and bake at 350 degrees until tender and well done. Add more water if needed.
Courtesy Duncan Gilchrist, Hamilton, Montana

WILD RABBIT

1 or 2 wild rabbits, cut up
Flour
Salt to taste
Pepper to taste
Shortening
1/4 cup water
1/4 cup wine
2 cans cream of mushroom soup
2 onions, sliced
Worcestershire sauce
Tabasco sauce
1 clove of garlic
1 bay leaf
2 or 3 strips bacon

Boil rabbit pieces for 1 hour. Dry thoroughly. Put flour, salt and pepper in bag; place rabbit pieces in bag and shake. Braise rabbit pieces in pressure cooker in small amount of shortening. Add water, wine, soup, onions, dash of Worcestershire sauce, dash of Tabasco sauce, garlic and bay leaf. Place strips of bacon over top. Close cooker and cook for 20 to 24 minutes. Yield: 4-6 servings.

BAKED PHEASANT

2-3 pheasant breasts
Flour
1/4 cup butter
1 can mushroom (or cream of chicken) soup
1 cup cream

Roll pheasant in flour and brown in butter. Place in a casserole dish. Mix soup and cream together and pour over browned pheasant. Bake at 275 degrees for 1 1/2 hours.

FRIED RABBIT

2 young 2 to 3 pound rabbits
2 egg yolks, beaten
3 cups milk
1 1/4 cups flour
Salt
1/2 cup fat
Pepper
2 teaspoons currant jelly
1 tablespoon minced parsley

Wash rabbits thoroughly and then dry. Cut into serving pieces. Combine egg yolks and 1 cup milk, gradually adding 1 cup flour. Add 1 teaspoonful salt and then beat until smooth. Dip rabbit into batter and then fry in fat for 15 minutes or until brown. Reduce heat; continue cooking for 30 to 40 minutes or until tender, turning frequently. Add remaining flour to fat in pan and then stir in remaining milk. Heat to boiling. Season to taste with salt and pepper. Garnish with jelly and parsley. Serves 6 to 8.

BAKED WILD GOOSE

1/2 chicken
Giblets of wild fowl
2 teaspoons salt
Water
1 cup chopped celery
1 cup chopped onions
1 large loaf bread, cut into bite-sized pieces
1 teaspoon (heaping) sage
1/2 teaspoon pepper
1 large wild goose

Combine chicken, giblets, 1 teaspoonful salt and 1 quart water in saucepan. Boil for 1 hour or until meat is tender. Remove meat from bones and then chop meat and giblets into bite-sized pieces. Combine celery and onions in sauce pan with boiling water to cover. Boil for 15-20 minutes. Add celery mixture to meat mixture and then combine bread, sage, remaining salt and pepper with celery and meat mixture. Stuff fowl with dressing. Cover and bake at 300 degrees for 2 hours. Then uncover and bake for 15 minutes to brown. Note: You can remove wild tase by putting a few bacon slices across breast of the goose during the last 15 minutes of baking. Also, you can substitute 2 or 3 wild ducks for the goose in recipe. Serves 8-10.

ROAST WILD DUCK

1 wild duck
Salt to taste
1/4 teaspoon allspice
1/4 teaspoon cloves
1 medium onion
Flour
1/2 cup water
1 recipe favorite stuffing
2 strips bacon

Clean duck. Thoroughly salt inside and out. Refrigerate for 24 hours. Rub skin of duck with allspice and cloves and then place onion inside cavity of duck. Roll duck in flour and then place in roaster; pour in water. Cover tightly and bake at 350 degrees for 1 hour. Remove and discard onion. Stuff duck with favorite dressing. Replace duck in roaster. Lay 2 strips of bacon over breast of duck; baste with drippings. Bake at 300 degrees for 1 hour and 30 minutes. Broth may be thickened for gravy, if desired. Yield: 2 servings.

OVEN-FRIED QUAIL

6 quail
1/2 cup herb stuffing mix, crushed
1/3 cup grated Parmesan cheese
2 tablespoons finely chopped green onion
1/3 cup butter or margarine, melted

Preheat oven to 350 degrees. Line 2-inch-deep baking pan with heavy duty aluminum foil. Split quail down back and flatten. Combine stuffing mix, cheese and onion. Dip quail in melted butter and then coat with stuffing mixture. Place in pan and bake for 30 to 35 minutes for small quail, 35 to 40 minutes for large quail, or until meat can be removed easily from bone. Serve immediately. Makes 3 servings.

BAKED QUAIL

1 onion, diced
4 tablespoons butter
4 cups toasted bread cubes
1 can cream of mushroom soup
2 eggs, beaten
Salt and pepper to taste
8 quail
8 strips bacon

Saute onion in butter. Add soup, eggs, bread cubes, salt and pepper. Stuff quail with dressing. Then wrap each bird with strip of bacon. Place quail in baking pan. Pour in small amount of water. Bake at 350 degrees for 1 hour and 30 minutes. Serves 8.

PHEASANT BREAST

1 pheasant breast
Flour
Salt to taste
Pepper to taste
Shortening

Slice pheasant breast into strips 1/4 inch thick, slicing parallel to breast bone. Begin at side and work to centerbone, doing both sides. Blend flour with salt and pepper. Roll strips in seasoned flour. Use a heavy fry pan at about 425 degrees. Brush pan with shortening until well covered and fry strips for 10 to 15 minutes, turning once. Makes 4 servings.

FRIED WILD DUCK

2-3 duck breasts
Solution (1 quart water/1 tablespoon salt)
Flour
Butter
1 onion, finely chopped
Salt and pepper
Garlic salt

Soak duck breast in salt solution for 1 hour. Rinse. Cut breasts into 2 pieces. Flour. Then place in frying pan or on griddle over medium heat and cook slowly in butter until browned. Add onion, salt, pepper and garlic salt. Simmer 30 minutes.

BISON POT ROAST

3 pound Bison roast
2 tablespoons cooking oil
1 bay leaf
1 teaspoon salt
5 peppercorns
4 carrots, sliced
5 spanish onions
5 potatoes, peeled/quartered
1 stalk celery, chopped
1 cup apple juice
1 cup water
1/2 teaspoon pepper
1 tablespoon cornstarch

Pre-heat oven to 300 degrees. Heat oil in Dutch oven over medium heat. Add bison roast and brown well on all sides. Add onions, carrots, celery, bay leaf, salt, pepper, apple juice and water. Cover and place in preheated oven for 1 hour. Remove from oven, add potatoes. Cover and return to oven for 1 hour or until potatoes are fork tender. Thicken gravy with cornstarch.

•Cook a frozen bison roast at 275 degrees allowing 1/3 to 1/2 additional cooking time.

•Remove roasts from oven at about 5 degrees under-done and allow to "set" for 15-30 minutes, depending on size.

BISON ROAST LEFTOVERS

A Bison roast is like any other meat roast — it is usually more meat than is needed for one meal. Leftover Bison meat may be sliced, cubed, diced or ground. It can be substituted for beef in almost any recipe. It is also delicious if sliced thin and served cold!

EASY BISON CHICKEN FRIED STEAK

4 1-pound Bison burger patties
2 eggs, slightly beaten
1/2 cup flour, 1 teaspoon salt, 1/4 teaspoon pepper
1/3 cup cooking oil

Combine flour, salt, and pepper in bowl. Dip burger patties in egg mixture, covering both sides then dip in flour mixture, covering both sides. Brown meat slowly on both sides in hot oil in large skillet. Cover with tight fitting lid, cook over low heat 30-45 minutes. Remove meat to platter and keep warm.

Gravy:
3 tablespoons flour
1/8 teaspoon pepper
1/2 teaspoon salt
1 1/2 cups light cream (milk)

To drippings in skillet, add flour, salt and pepper, stirring to loosen brown bits on pan bottom. Add 1 1/2 cups cream or milk and cook over low heat, stirring constantly, until mixture thickens.

GRILLED BISON STEAK

Steaks recommended for grilling/barbecuing include Rib Eyes, T-Bones and New York Strips. Cooking time is important in order not to overcook your steaks. Total cooking time will depend on the thickness of the steaks:

1" thick - Rare 6 - 8 minutes   Med: 10 - 12 min.
1 1/2 " thick - Rare: 10 - 12 min.   Med. 14 - 18 min.
2" thick - Rare: 14 - 10 min   Med: 20 - 25 min.
Note: Well Done Bison steaks are not recommended. Due to the leanness of the meat, Bison has a tendency to become dry when overcooked.

GROUND BISON

Bison burger may be used as a substitute in any of your recipes calling for ground beef. Bison will be leaner than any ground steak or burger you are accustomed to and precautions must be taken in order for it not to dry out. Do not expect it to shrink or leave any residues in the pan after cooking. Although Bison burger is leaner, additional fat is not recommended when preparing a recipe. This will only increase the amount of fat and cholesterol you are trying to avoid.

HOT AND SPICY
BISON MEAT BALLS
AND CRANBERRY SAUCE

2 pounds Bison burger
1 egg
Finely diced onion
1 16-ounce can jellied cranberry sauce
3 tablespoons prepared horseradish
1 tablespoon Worchestershire sauce
1 clove garlic (minced)
2 tablespoons honey
1 tablespoon lemon juice
1/2 teaspoon ground red pepper

Add beaten egg to bison burger, mix well. Form into bite size bison balls. Brown in oil (or use microwave). In medium sauce pan, combine cranberry sauce, horseradish, honey, Worcestershire, lemon juice, garlic and red pepper. Bring to boil, reduce heat and simmer covered for 5 minutes. Add meatballs and serve.

•To keep the shape of meatballs, plunge momentarily into rapidly boiling water before cooking. This will also seal in the flavor.

BROILED BISON STEAK

Rub your favorite cut of steak with a combination of a little garlic salt, cooking oil, ground black pepper and lemon juice. The lemon will make it tangy, and gives zippy flavor.

•Do not use a fork to turn steaks, this punctures the meat allowing the juices to escape.

•Lesser quality Bison steaks are not recommended for grilling unless they have been marinated.

•For good cooking, preheat broiler at least 5 minutes before you broil a steak.

•Steaks thinner than 3/4 inches thick are not recommended for barbecuing or broiling.

GRILLED BISON ROAST

3-4 pound Top Round Bison roast
Seasoned salt

Rub all sides of roast well with seasoned salt. Place in pan and set at room temperature for 30 minutes. Use a rotisserie or grill on flat surface at moderate heat. Roast will be done at 130 degrees (use meat thermometer). Remove from heat immediately and set aside for 15 minutes before carving. (Note: the quality of meat will decrease rapidly at temperatures above 130 degrees.) Turn every 20 minutes when grilling on flat surface being careful not to puncture the outer crust.

BISON ROAST

The most acceptable cooking methods for preparing the perfect Bison roast is low temperature and high moisture. Using a meat thermometer is the best way to insure that you don't overcook the meat. The best oven temperature for preparing a Bison roast is at 275 degrees, cooked to the desired internal doneness. Covering the roast in aluminum foil or using a roasting bag helps retain the juices during cooking.

CROCK POT BISON ROAST

3-4 pound boneless Bison chuck roast (frozen)
Seasonings to taste (salt, pepper, garlic, onion, etc.)

Place frozen roast in crock pot. Add seasonings to 1/2 cup of water and pour over roast. Cook on low setting about 8 to 12 hours or until bison is fork-tender. Slice and serve with drippings, au jus style, or with gravy made from drippings. Leftovers make good French dip sandwiches.

BISON ROAST IN FOIL

3-4 pound roast
1/2 envelope dry onion soup mix

Preheat oven to 325 degrees. Place roast on an ample piece of heavy duty aluminum foil. Sprinkle 1/2 envelope of dry onion soup mix over the meat. Bring edges of foil together. Add 1/2 cup water and seal tightly. Place in shallow roasting pan and bake at 275 degrees for 2 to 4 hours or until internal temperature reaches desired doneness. 1/2 hour before completion, 1/2 cup of wine may be added for a special flavor. Save the juices and thicken for gravy.

BISON FAJITAS

Fajitas are a Mexican dish using the skirt, flank or round steak which is marinated, cooked and served on a flour tortilla with onions, tomato, green pepper, sour cream, guacamole, and hot sauce.

1 pound Bison skirt, flank or round steak (cut 1/2 inch thick slices)
Marinade:
Juice of 2-3 limes
1/2 teaspoon garlic salt
1/2 teaspoon pepper
(or buy fajita marinade at your local grocery)

Garnishes:
1 large tomato, chopped
3 green onions, chopped
1 large green pepper, sliced
Guacamole
Sour Cream
Picante sauce

4 flour or corn tortillas, warmed

Pound meat into 1/2 inch thickness. Place steak slices in plastic bag; sprinkle both sides of steak with lime juice, garlic salt and pepper. Tie bag securely and marinate in refrigerator 6-8 hours. Drain marinade, broil meat over medium high mesquite coals 2-3 minutes on each side. Carve into thin slices, serve in warmed flour or corn tortillas. Add garnishes as desired. Serves 4.

BISON PITA POCKETS

1 pound Sirloin Bison steak
1 medium cucumber, peeled and grated
1 cup low-fat plain yogurt
3 cloves garlic
2 medium tomatoes
1 sweet green pepper, chopped
4 pita pockets
Salt and pepper to taste

Squeeze excess liquid from grated cucumber; mix with yogurt and garlic, set aside. Broil meat for 4-5 minutes per side. Slice cooked meat, thinly across the grain. Fill pita pockets with meat, tomatoes, and green pepper; add yogurt sauce and season with salt and pepper. Serves 4.

BISON WITH BROCCOLI STIR-FRY

1 pound Bison steak (flank, top round, sirloin) cut into 1/8" slices
1 1/2 cups broccoli stems cut in 1/8" slices
2 1/2 cups broccoli florets
1/4 pound fresh mushrooms, 1/8" slices
1 large onion, chopped
2 large cloves garlic (crushed)
3 tablespoons peanut oil
2 teaspoons corn starch, 1/3 cup water, 1 beef bouillon cube
3/4 teaspoon sugar, 2 tablespoons cider vinegar, 1/3 cup soy sauce
Chinese noodles or rice

Mix together soy sauce, vinegar and sugar. In another bowl, mix bouillon, water and corn starch. (As with all stir-fry recipes, all cutting and chopping must be done in advance!)

In heavy large skillet or wok: Add 1 1/2 tablespoons peanut oil (med-hi heat), add garlic to heating oil. Add meat and stir-fry 2 minutes or until medium brown but pink in center. Remove meat and pan juices. Add 1 tablespoon peanut oil, when hot, add onion and broccoli stems, stir fry 2 minutes until crisp and tender. Add remaining oil around edge of skillet or wok, add broccoli florets and mushrooms, stir-fry 2 minutes. Pour in meat pan juices and soy sauce, vinegar, sugar mixture. Stir and cover. Cook 2 minutes. Stir corn starch/bouillon mixture and pour into skillet or wok. Cook stirring constantly 2-3 minutes until thickened. Serve over chinese noodles or rice and enjoy! Serves 4.

BAR-B-QUE BISON

4-5 pound Bison chuck roast

Pat the sides and top of a chuck roast with brown sugar. Wrap in foil and cook 10 hours at 225-250 degrees. Separate into large chunks. Combine cooking juices with the following sauce and marinate meat for 4 hours.

Barbecue Sauce: Simmer 15 minutes
3/4 cup ketchup
1/4 cup butter
2 tablespoons mustard
1 tablespoon Worcestershire sauce
2 tablespoons brown sugar
1 teaspoon salt
1 raw onion, sliced

Serve on toasted, buttered buns and top with grated cheese.

BISON LASAGNA

1 pound Bison burger
1 clove garlic, minced
1 6-ounce can tomato paste
1 tablespoon basil
1 1/2 teaspoons salt

To prepare meat filling, brown burger with garlic, basil & salt. Add tomato paste and simmer uncovered for 30 minutes.

Cheese filling:
3 cups cottage cheese
1/2 cup grated parmesan cheese
1 pound mozzarella cheese
2 tablespoons parsley flakes
2 beaten eggs
1/2 teaspoon pepper
2 teaspoon salt

Slice mozzarella cheese. Prepare lasagna noodles as directed on package. Place 1/2 of the prepared noodles in bottom of 13x9 inch pan. Over noodles, spread 1/2 cheese filling, 1/2 meat filling, 1/2 sliced mozzarella. Lay the rest of the noodles over mozzarella and repeat the procedure. Bake at 375 F for 30 minutes. Let set for 40 minutes before cutting.

Editor's Note: *We are indebted to the American Bison Association for permission to use some of their recipes in this book. They have a publication available that provides some additional recipes utilizing bison and you can reach them at American Bison Association, P.O. Box 16660, Denver, CO 80216.*

IT AIN'T STEW WITHOUT A RUTABAGA

Shortly after dawn that cold November morning in 1990, and some ten minutes after I'd come across the elk tracks in the new snow, I knew that to hunt them properly I'd have to climb to the ridgetop where I'd be exposed to the bitter-cold wind that was pushing the blizzard in from the north. That was the precise opposite of what I had planned for the day, which had been to do exactly what the elk had done — skirt the bottom of the open ridge and ease into the timber on the northslope of the opposite ridge and climb comfortably to the big mountain at the back of the canyon, in the shelter of the timber, out of the storm.

There were at least fifteen or sixteen elk in the herd and their tracks hadn't even begun to drift in despite the intensity of the snowstorm. Fresh tracks! Incredibly fresh, made just moments before, an elk hunter's dream with at least two certain and possibly a third bull tracks showing in the snow. Obviously the herd had moved, at daylight, from the meadows below and climbed unhurriedly to the shelter of the heavily-timbered north slope where they'd spend the day, out of the wind, chewing their cud and letting the blizzard blow over them.

Now this ridge lifted steeply from the grasslands at the valley bottom and climbed southwesterly for about four and a half miles, dotted here and there by clumps of several spindly Douglas fir trees huddling together in a sea of south-slope grass that now only poked occasionally through an unbroken cover of snow. My object would be to climb to the backbone of the ridge, which paralleled the opposite, south, ridge to the headway still some four miles away. I would need that altitude to have a chance at spying the elk before they realized I was there; otherwise, with time running out on the season, I might not get an opportunity to take a bull in this district where only adult, brow-tined bulls could be taken.

I hurried up the mountain, climbing and scrambling as best I could in the deepening snow and the increasing intensity of the blizzard but it took me almost two hours just to get to the backbone of the ridge. By then, I knew, the elk would already be bedded somewhere under the dense canopy of the canyon below me or along the opposite, equally steep ridge that was occasionally obscured by the swirling snow.

For another hour or two, I eased along the open ridgetop, stopping occasionally to clean snow from my Leupold 7x35 field glasses and study the forested slope to the south. Somewhere along that steep mountain I would, I was sure, come across the herd of elk, if I could only hold out against the incredible cold long enough to catch up to the elk and maybe, just maybe, get a shot at a bull. To accomplish that I had no choice but to work my way along the top of the ridge where I was totally exposed to the shrieking wind; sure, I could escape the stinging cold by dropping a hundred feet or so off either side of the ridge, but if I succumbed to the desire for comfort I would give up my commanding view of the south ridge.

Fortunately, my hunter's instinct to keep the advantage of the high ground prevailed long after I was not only numbingly cold but beginning to feel the pangs of hunger. Another hour of strenuous, slow climbing through the now knee-deep snow brought me to one of those clumps of twisted Douglas fir trees and I decided I'd stop there, dig into my daybag, and take out a sandwich and have some lunch. Maybe that would help generate some body heat because now, perspiring heavily from the laborious climb while being literally blasted by the incessant wind and the sharp sting of the snow hitting the exposed skin on my face, I realized I had truly become very chilled and that my body wasn't regenerating the body heat I was expending.

The notion of lunch, however, lasted only a few jerky seconds as I eased under the twisted fir, knelt in the snow and shook the daybag off my back. I stripped off my gloves and, with stiff fingers, unbuckled the flap on the daybag — just as my eyes caught a slight movement some two hundred yards across the canyon and I realized that I was being watched by a cow elk who had been feeding in a small opening just opposite me.

Immediately I spied several elk, seven in all — five cows and two calves of the season. They had seen me, sure enough. The lead cow and another mature cow were standing with heads alert, looking directly at me, but neither they nor any of the others seemed alarmed. Then they went back to feeding and within minutes I counted another nine elk, all cows and calves, interspersed through the trees. But no bulls.

A half an hour passed and, finally, I began to shiver uncontrollably as the howling wind increased. Cold, hungry, frustrated, I watched helplessly as the elk across the canyon split into two groups; one, a band of six or seven, (I couldn't be sure) ambled out of sight around the far ridge to the right. The other, uphill group walked into a clump of fir and suddenly I was alone on the hill.

I knew better, however, but as that last cow elk disappeared into the trees I suddenly became both more cold and more hungry and the storm seemed even more severe than it had been at any time across the day. I heard myself say, quietly, aloud: "Man, I sure could use a bowl of old Omer Julien's stew right now."

Stew! That sounded both warm and good. The thought overwhelmed me. But Omer Julien's stew! Now that was something real special and it had to be a cruel trick for my subconscious mind to raise the thought of his wonderful, famous, wilderness stew at a time like this. More than thirty years had passed since I'd last enjoyed a meal of Omer Julien's stew when I was working, as a young man, for him and his partner as a hunting guide in their camp on the edge of the Bob Marshall Wilderness. Rich, thick, tasty, his stew was famed among those who traveled the trails of the Bob Marshall Wilderness and the Spotted Bear country; many was the time, in that camp, that we'd hear a string of horses pull off the main trail and come down to camp to get a bowl or two of Omer's famous stew.

And as I stood there, shivering and yet unwilling to give up the chance at an elk, I could both smell that incredible stew and hear Omer Julien say, as he always did, that, "Heck, it ain't nothin' special. It's the rutabagas that give it the taste. It ain't stew if there ain't rutabagas in it."

I slipped a spoonful of that stew to my mouth, savoring its mingled, warm smell of potatoes, carrots, elk meat, onions, and, of course, rutabagas, and my mind sped back across those thirty years since I'd even seen Omer Julien, let alone eaten a bowlful of his stew, and marveled at the power of the human mind to recall such things at times like I found myself in that raw, cold, hunting day.

Then, an almost startling revelation hit me. I KNEW why my subconscious mind had brought the memory of Omer Julien's stew to my conscious mind: the need of the moment demanded it. Once, in that hunting camp some thirty years earlier, over a bowl of stew, Omer Julien had told me of a technique he used on occasion when hunting alone and need demanded it: the making of a one-man elk drive. The situation I now found myself in demanded exactly that sort of technique. I was alone. I had to make the elk across the canyon to my left move out of the timber and cross the notch at the end of the ridge so I could both see them and, possibly, get a shot at a bull. For there was, I was still sure, at least one and maybe two bulls hidden in that timber across the canyon. And I also was sure that some of the elk that had just walked into that timber were still watching me.

So, still savoring a bite of stew I hadn't really had, I executed Omer Julien's one-man elk drive — to perfection. His concept is simply this: you stride openly and directly straight, in full view of the elk, toward them for twenty to thirty yards, hoping to force them to begin moving in a specific direction without driving them to a run. Then, you immediately go backwards in your own tracks until you're out of sight — and then run like crazy to a predetermined spot to get in position to make a shot as the elk move toward where you're supposedly driving them.

I did just as Omer said. I strode out in the open toward the elk, staring in the open space of the canyon between us and thinking this idea is crazy, back-tracked until I got back to the clump of trees, and then scrambled like a madman for a couple of hundred yards on up the ridge — just in time to intercept nine elk, walking resolutely in single-file, toward the pass that led into the canyon on the north side of the ridge I'd climbed. Two of the elk were bulls, the third in the line a small raghorn and the seventh a huge six-pointer with a massive body. He was exactly the sort of bull I'd hoped for and, seconds later, I had my elk, that nice six-pointer, thanks in no large part to a bowl of stew, with a rutabaga in it — and some advice that had been given me thirty years earlier about how to accomplish a one-man elk drive. It was, unquestionably, one of the best meals I ever had.

SALADS

TUNA/RICE SALAD

1 1/2 cups water
2 chicken bouillon cubes
1 1/2 cups instant rice
1/2 cup chopped celery
1/2 cup frozen peas
2 tablespoons parsley or 1 teaspoon dried parsley flakes
1 can tuna, drained and flaked
3/4 cup mayonnaise
2 tablespoons lemon juice

Bring water to boil and add bouillon cubes and rice. Let stand until water is absorbed, usually 5 or 6 minutes. Mix remaining ingredients thoroughly with hot rice. Then chill for several hours. Use same ingredients and procedure for shrimp salad, simply replacing tuna with shrimp.

BROCCOLI SALAD

1 bunch broccoli, chopped
2 cups chopped celery
1 green pepper, chopped
1 can sliced mushrooms, drained
1 can ripe olives, sliced
1 can water chestnuts, diced
1 box cherry tomatoes, cut in half
1 (8 ounce) bottle Zesty Italian dressing
1 package dry Italian dressing mix

Toss all together, mixing thoroughly. Cool or refrigerate. A good camp salad because it keeps well.

SHELL MACARONI/HAM SALAD

2 cups diced cooked ham
1 cup diced American cheese
4 - 5 cups cooked shell macaroni
4 hard-cooked eggs, diced
1 cup diced celery
1/2 cup diced pimento
1/4 cup diced green pepper
2 tablespoons sugar
1 cup salad dressing
1/4 to 1/2 cup diced onion
1/2 teaspoon salt
1/4 teaspoon pepper
1/4 teaspoon paprika
3 tablespoons sweet pickle relish
1 tablespoon lemon juice

Mix all ingredients together, stirring thoroughly. Chill several hours or overnight. Makes 15 to 18 servings.

CUCUMBER/ONION SALAD

1 large cucumber, sliced
1 onion, sliced and ringed
1 cup sour cream
2 tablespoons vinegar
Salt and pepper

Mix sour cream and vinegar together and stir into cucumber and onion slices. Salt and pepper to taste. Best if cooled or refrigerate for several hours.

SHRIMP SALAD

1 1/2 tablespoons unflavored gelatin
1/2 cup cold water
1 cup tomato soup
2 ounces cream cheese
1 can shrimp
1 cup mayonnaise
1 cup finely chopped celery
1 teaspoon grated onion
1 tablespoon grated green pepper

Soften gelatin in water and then dissolve in hot tomato soup. Cool and add the remaining ingredients, mixing thoroughly. Cool overnight in refrigerator or icebox. Serves 10 to 12.

BAKED CHICKEN SALAD

3 cups chopped cooked chicken
1 1/2 cups celery slices
1 cup (4 ounces) shredded sharp Cheddar cheese
1 tablespoon chopped onion
1 tablespoon lemon juice
1 1/2 teaspoons salt
Dash of pepper
Salad dressing
Tomato slices
1 1/2 cups crushed potato chips

Combine chicken, celery, 1/2 cup cheese, onion, lemon juice, seasonings and enough salad dressing to moisten. Mix lightly and then spoon into 1 1/2 quart casserole and top with tomatoes. Bake at 350 degrees for 35 to 40 minutes. Top with combined remaining cheese and chips and continue baking until cheese is melted. 6 servings.

MACARONI SALAD

1 medium package salad macaroni, cooked
1 can tuna, drained and flaked
4 hard-cooked eggs, chopped
1/3 cup chopped dill pickle
1/4 cup chopped green onions
3 or 4 chopped radishes
2 stalks celery, chopped
1/2 teaspoon celery seed
Salt
Pepper
1 cup mayonnaise
1/4 cup dill pickle juice

Combine ingredients and mix well. Chill until ready to serve. Sweet pickles and sweet pickle juice may be substituted for dill for a different taste. A great side dish that serves 6 to 8.

SPECIAL SALAD DRESSING

4 tablespoons sugar
1 teaspoon pepper
2 teaspoon soy sauce
1 teaspoon salt
1/2 cup oil
1/2 cup rice vinegar

Combine above ingredients to make the dressing. Pour over salad just before serving.

LAYERED SALAD

1/2 pound bacon, cooked crisp and crumbled
1 head lettuce, chopped
1/2 cup chopped celery
1/2 cup green pepper
1 (10 ounce) package frozen peas
1 red onion, sliced
2 cups mayonnaise
2 tablespoons sugar
4 ounces cheddar cheese, grated

Layer with lettuce on bottom and your choice with celery, green pepper, peas and onion. Mix mayonnaise and sugar together and spread over layered vegetables, sealing edges before topping with bacon crumbs and grated cheddar cheese. Refrigerate or cool at least overnight.

FRUIT SALAD

2 bananas, diced
1 20-ounce can pineapple chunks, drained
1 11-ounce can mandarin oranges, drained
1 16-ounce can fruit cocktail, keep juice
2 apples, diced
1 small jar maraschino cherries, drain and slice
1 package instant vanilla pudding mix

Mix the fruit together. Then mix 1 cup fruit cocktail juice, adding water to make 1 cup if necessary, with pudding mix to dissolve. Mix thoroughly with fruit and allow to set 10 or 15 minutes to blend flavors.

HOT CHICKEN SALAD

4 cups chopped cooked chicken
4 cups celery, chopped
2 teaspoons salt
1/2 teaspoon tarragon, (optional)
1/4 cup grated onion
1 tablespoon lemon juice
2 cups mayonnaise
1/4 cup extra dry Vermouth
1 cup sliced, blanched, toasted almonds
1 cup crushed corn flakes
1/2 cup freshly grated Parmesan or Romano cheese

Thoroughly combine chicken and celery with salt, tarragon, grated onion, lemon juice, mayonnaise, Vermouth and toasted almonds. Allow to stand at least 1 hour. Taste and add additional salt if desired. Spoon into a buttered shallow baking dish. Top with crushed corn flakes and freshly grated Parmesan or Romano cheese. Place in a 350 degree oven for 25 to 30 minutes or until heated through and lightly browned. Approximately 12 to 15 servings.

CABBAGE SALAD

1 head shredded cabbage
3 green olives, chopped
4 ounces slivered almonds
1 package dry noodles, crumbled

Mix above ingredients together in a bowl.

SANDWICHES

CHICKEN SPREAD

1 3- to 4-pound hen
1 medium sized onion
2 carrots
1 cup chopped celery
1 hard-boiled egg
1/2 cup mayonnaise
1/2 cup salad dressing
Onion juice
Salt

In a medium-sized pan, boil one 3 or 4-pound hen with 1 onion and 2 carrots until tender. Add 2 tablespoons salt. Cover the chicken with water and cook very slowly. Cool chicken. Take the meat off and grind the meat. Discard the bones. Add about 1/2 cup of mayonnaise, 1/2 cup salad dressing, 1 cup chopped celery (very fine), a little onion juice, and a hard-boiled egg chopped into fine pieces and then mix all this together. Makes an excellent sandwich spread.

LEFT-OVER ROAST

2 cups ground roast
1/3 cup chopped onion
1 cup salad dressing
1/2 cup ground sweet pickles
2 hard-boiled eggs (optional)
1/2 teaspoon salt

Mix together and spread on bread. This is another excellent way to make left-over items go farther. You can also cut up left-over steak to take the place of the roast left-overs.

TUNA SPREAD

1 small can tuna or other canned fish
1/3 cup mayonnaise
1/3 cup salad dressing
1/2 cup chopped celery
Juice of 1/2 a lemon

Mix together and spread on bread. This can easily be fixed at home or in camp. We like to prepare it daily so freshness is guaranteed.

CUCUMBER SPREAD

1 6-ounce package cream cheese
1 small, firm cucumber

Chop cucumber in small pieces. Then mix thoroughly and spread on bread.

SPAM SPREAD

1 can Spam, ground or cut to very fine pieces
1/2 cup salad dressing
2 hard-boiled eggs, chopped fine
1/2 teaspoon salt
1/3 cup chopped sweet pickle

Mix together and spread on bread.

BISON SANDWICH FILLING

1 cup cooked bison roast (ground)
1 tablespoon minced onion
1 tablespoon pickle relish
1 tablespoon lemon juice
2 tablespoons salad dressing
1/2 teaspoon salt
1/8 teaspoon black pepper
Softened butter
8 slices bread

Grind leftover Bison roast in meat grinder. Combine the first 7 ingredients — if too dry to stick together, add a bit of cream or evaporated milk. Spread bread slices with butter and divide filling for 4 sandwiches. For a variation, add 1-2 chopped hard cooked eggs to filling mixture.

MINI-QUICHES

1 can refrigerated dinner rolls
1 package ham and cheese spread
2 eggs, chopped
2 green onions with tops, chopped

Separate rolls into 12 pieces. Divide each piece into 3 sections. Press sections in tart or muffin cups (small); stretch dough to form shell. Combine cheese spread, eggs and onion, mix well. Divide mixture evenly among shells. Bake in 375 degree oven for 15 minutes.

SNACKS

HIGH-NUTRITION SQUARES

1/2 cup firmly packed brown sugar
1/2 cup light or dark molasses
1/2 cup vegetable shortening
3/4 cup water
1 cup raisins
1 cup chopped pitted dates
3 eggs
2 cups whole wheat flour
1/2 cup wheat germ
1 teaspoon baking soda
1 teaspoon baking powder
2 teaspoons cinnamon
1/2 teaspoon mace
1/2 teaspoon cloves

Combine brown sugar, molasses, shortening, water, raisins and dates in a medium-sized pan and then bring mixture to boiling. Remove from heat and allow to cool to room temperature. Then beat in eggs until smooth. Stir in remaining ingredients and beat with a large spoon until smooth. Pour mixture into greased 9 inch square pan and bake in preheated oven at 350 degrees for 40 to 45 minutes. Then set pan on a wire rack and cool. Cut to size desired.

GRANOLA BARS

6 cups granola
1/2 cup walnuts, chopped
1/2 cup coconut
1/2 cup raisins
1 1/2 cups brown sugar
1 1/2 sticks butter or margarine
3/4 cup dark corn syrup
1/2 cup honey

2 squares chocolate
1/2 cup peanut butter
1 teaspoon vanilla
1/2 teaspoon baking soda

Mix granola, walnuts, coconut and raisins in a large bowl and set aside. Then boil brown sugar, butter, corn syrup, honey and chocolate in saucepan for 4 to 5 minutes, stirring frequently. Remove from heat and add peanut butter, vanilla and baking soda. Stir thoroughly and pour over granola mixture. Stir until well mixed. Pour into buttered 9x13x2" pan and pat down evenly. Allow to cool. Cut into pieces and wrap in plastic wrap. This is a great high-energy snack with extra-special taste especially recommended for taking along on day hikes and hunting trips.

ENERGY SNACK BAR

3/4 cup butter or shortening
1/4 cup brown sugar
1/4 cup honey
1/2 cup molasses
2 eggs
1 cup 7-grain quick-cooking cereal
1/2 cup coconut
2 1/2 cups all-purpose flour
1 teaspoon baking powder
1/2 teaspoon cinnamon
1/4 teaspoon allspice
1/4 teaspoon cloves
1/4 teaspoon salt

Cream butter and sugar and then blend in honey, molasses and eggs. Add remaining ingredients and mix thoroughly. Drop by tablespoonful onto ungreased cookie sheet and bake at 375 degrees for 12 to 15 minutes. You'll find this to be an excellent energy booster on cold days.

BUTTERSCOTCH SNACK

6 cups dry breakfast cereal (corn flakes or similar dry cereal)
1/2 cup brown sugar
1 cup dry roasted peanuts
1 cup raisins
6 ounces butterscotch chips
1/2 cup melted margarine or butter

Mix all dry ingredients in large bowl. Pour melted margarine over the mixture and mix thoroughly until completely crumbly. Spread on a cookie sheet and dry in oven with oven door ajar, at about 150 degrees, until butterscotch chips are melted and the mix is crispy.

HUNTER'S GORP

Mix 1 cup raisins with 1/2 cup banana chips and 1/4 cup peanuts. Makes about 2 cups. Options vary as wide as your taste — chocolate (or carab) chips, M&M candies, dried fruit (apricots, apples, etc.). Makes a great, high-energy snack in camp or on a day's outing.

FRUIT DIP

1 -ounce jar marshmallow creme
1 8-ounce package cream cheese

Mix together and serve chilled with fresh fruit. You can also add a few dashes of nutmeg or a small can of pineapple for variations.

SOUPS

VEGETABLE BEEF SOUP

3 pounds beef soup bones
3 quarts cold water
1 tablespoon salt
1 bay leaf
2 sprigs parsley
4 celery tops
1 onion, quartered
1 1-pound can tomatoes
1 cup diced potatoes
4 stalks celery, sliced
3 carrots, sliced
1 10-ounce package frozen mixed vegetables
1 cup alphabet noodles or barley

Cover meat with cold water, add seasonings, parsley, celery tops and onion. Bring to boil and skim if needed. Cover and simmer 3 hours or until meat is tender. Remove bay leaf and soup bones. Cut meat from bones, returning to soup along with remaining ingredients. Cover and simmer 45 to 50 minutes or until vegetables are tender. Makes 6 to 8 servings.

BUTTER BEAN SOUP

1 can (15 ounces) butter beans
1 16-ounce can stewed tomatoes
3 tablespoons butter or margarine
1 tablespoon instant minced onion
1 1/2 teaspoons sugar
1/4 teaspoon seasoned salt
Dash pepper

Combine all ingredients in a saucepan and simmer for 30 to 40 minutes. Makes 3 to 4 servings.

EASY-TO-MAKE CHOWDER

2 cups boiling water
2 cups chopped potatoes
1/2 cup carrot slices
1/2 cup celery slices
1/4 cup chopped onion
1 1/2 teaspoons salt
1/4 teaspoon pepper
1/4 cup margarine
1/4 cup flour
2 cups milk
2 1/2 cups (10 ounces) shredded sharp natural cheddar cheese
1 17-ounce can cream style corn

Combine water, vegetables and seasonings. Cover and allow to simmer for 10 to 15 minutes. Do not drain. Make a white sauce with margarine, flour and milk. Add cheese, stir until melted. Then add corn and undrained vegetables. Heat but do not boil. Makes 6 to 8 servings.

VEGETABLE BEAN SOUP

1/2 cup chopped onion
2 tablespoons butter or margarine
1/2 pound wieners, sliced
1 16-ounce can mixed vegetables
2 cups tomato juice
1 cup water
1 teaspoon instant beef bouillon
1 teaspoon sugar

Saute onions in butter. Add remaining ingredients and simmer 30 to 40 minutes. Makes 6 servings.

BARLEY SOUP

2 pounds soup bones
2 tablespoons vegetable oil
2 quarts water
1 16-ounce can tomatoes, undrained
2 tablespoons fresh chopped parsley (or 2 teaspoons dried parsley flakes)
2 teaspoons salt
1/4 teaspoon pepper
1 cup diced carrots
1/2 cup chopped celery
1/4 cup chopped onion
2/3 cup pearled barley
1 cup fresh or frozen peas

In large saucepot or Dutch oven, brown soup bones in hot oil and then drain. Add water, tomatoes, parsley, salt and pepper. Bring to a boil; reduce heat. Add remaining ingredients except peas. Simmer, uncovered, about 60 minutes or until meat and barley are tender. Remove soup bones from broth. Strip meat from bones and return meat to broth. Add peas; continue simmering about 10 minutes. Makes 8 servings.

BASIC CREAM SOUP
(Low Cholesterol)

2 tablespoons minced onion
1/4 cup soft margarine
1/4 cup flour
3 1/2 cups frozen polyunsaturated non-dairy creamer
1 1/2 cups chopped or sieved cooked vegetables and vegetable liquid
Carrots, cauliflower, beans, broccoli

In a heavy saucepan, over low heat, cook onion and margarine until tender but not brown. Add flour and stir until smooth. Remove from heat and add 3 1/2 cups non-dairy creamer. Stir until smooth. Shortly before serving add vegetables of your choosing. Makes 6 servings.

FRENCH ONION SOUP

4 large onions, thinly sliced
1/4 pound butter or margarine
4 tablespoons butter
4 tablespoons all-purpose flour
2 cups beef broth
2 quarts water
1 tablespoon soy sauce
1 1/2 teaspoons salt
1 1/2 teaspoons Tabasco sauce
1 teaspoon Kitchen Bouquet
1/2 teaspoon Worcestershire sauce
2 beef bouillon cubes
6 slices French bread
1 8-ounce package shredded Mozzarella cheese

Saute onions in 1/4 pound hot butter or margarine until clear. In large saucepan, melt 4 tablespoons butter. Blend in flour and cook over low heat, stirring constantly, until dark brown. Gradually stir in beef broth. Bring to a boil. Boil for 1 minute, stirring constantly. Add sauteed onions in butter, water, soy sauce, salt, Tabasco sauce, Kitchen Bouquet, Worcestershire sauce and bouillon cubes. Mix well. Bring to a boil. Then cover and simmer over low heat 30 minutes. Pour into 6 individual soup servers and place a slice of bread on top of each. Cover each with shredded cheese. Heat under broiler until cheese is golden and bubbly. Serve at once. Serves 6.

CHUNKY VEGETABLE SOUP

2 pounds hot or sweet Italian sausage, cut into 1/2" slices
1 large onion, chopped
1 clove garlic, minced
2 cans (13 3/4 ounces each) beef broth
1 jar (15 1/2 ounces) spaghetti sauce, any flavor
1 medium zucchini, cut into 1/4" slices
4 cups water
1 cup sliced celery
1 cup sliced carrots
1 1/2 teaspoons basil
Salt to taste
Pepper to taste
1 1/2 cups uncooked elbow macaroni, cooked and drained
Grated Parmesan cheese

In a large Dutch oven, brown sausage thoroughly on all sides. Add onion and garlic. Saute until onion is translucent; drain fat. Then add remaining ingredients except pasta and cheese. Simmer for 30 minutes. Add pasta and allow to simmer another 10 minutes. Serve soup with Parmesan cheese. Serves about 6.

ONION SOUP

6 large onions, sliced
2 cans consomme
1/2 cup cream
3 tablespoons flour
1/2 teaspoon salt
2 cups water

Fry onions until a golden brown and then add flour and brown another minute. Add the consomme, water and cook for 1/2 hour slowly. Then run through a sieve and bring to a boil. Add cream and soup is ready to serve.

OLD HOMESTEADER SOUP

1/2 pound ground beef
1/2 cup green pepper strips
1/2 cup chopped onion
2 tablespoons chili powder
2 cans (11 1/4 ounces each) condensed chili beef soup
1/2 cup water
1 can (16 ounces) tomatoes, cut up
1 can (about 15 1/2 ounces) kidney beans, undrained

In large saucepan, brown beef and cook green pepper and onion with chili powder until tender (use shortening if necessary). Stir to separate meat. Add remaining ingredients and let simmer for 15 to 20 minutes, stirring often. Serves six.

SPLIT PEA SOUP

1 ham hock or ham bone
2 quarts water
2 cups dried split peas
1 medium onion, sliced
2 sprigs parsley
1 bay leaf
1/4 teaspoon crumbled thyme
1/4 teaspoon crumbled marjoram
Dash cayenne
2 cups sliced carrot
2 cups sliced celery
Salt and pepper

Combine ham hock, water, peas, onion, parsley and seasonings and bring to boil. Cover and allow to simmer 2 hours or until peas are soft. Add carrot and celery. Cover and simmer 30 minutes or until vegetables are tender. Remove ham hock. Cut meat from bone and return to soup. Season to taste with salt and pepper. Six servings.

LOGGING CAMP VEGETABLE SOUP

3 pounds fresh tomatoes
2 1/2 quarts water or chicken broth
1 cup chopped onion
1 cup chopped celery
2 bay leaves
3 teaspoons basil leaves, divided
2 teaspoons salt
1/2 teaspoon ground black pepper
4 cups coarsely chopped cabbage
2 cups cauliflower flowerets
2 cups fresh corn kernels
2 cups sliced carrots
2 cups sliced zucchini
2 cups peeled, diced potatoes
Parsley flakes (optional)

Remove cores of tomatoes and coarsely chop. Place in a large pot with water; bring to a boil. Add onion and celery, bay leaves, 1 1/2 teaspoons basil, salt and black pepper. Cover and simmer for 1 hour. Add remaining vegetables. Cover and simmer until vegetables are tender, 50 to 60 minutes longer. Add remaining 1 1/2 teaspoons basil leaves; simmer 5 minutes longer. Sprinkle with parsley flakes, if desired.

LENTIL SOUP

1/2 pound lentils
4 cups cold water
1 ham hock or meaty ham bone
1/3 cup each chopped onion, celery and carrots
1 small bay leaf
1/2 teaspoon salt
1 small garlic clove, if desired

Wash and drain lentils. Combine all ingredients in kettle with tight-fitting lid. Bring to boil. Then reduce heat and simmer, covered, for 2 hours with occasional stirring. Remove ham hock or bone. Cut ham off bone, dice and add to soup and heat thoroughly. Remove bay leaf before serving. If soup is too thick, you can thin by adding water. Makes about 6 servings.

NEW ENGLAND CLAM CHOWDER

2 dozen shell clams or 2 cans (8 ounces each) minced clams
1 cup water
1/4 pound salt pork or bacon, minced
1/2 cup finely chopped onion
1 1/2 cups clam liquor, plus water
5 cups diced potatoes
2 cups milk
8 saltine crackers
2 cups half and half
2 tablespoons margarine or butter
Chopped parsley

Wash clam shells thoroughly. Place clams in a large pot with 1 cup water. Bring to a boil and simmer for 5 to 8 minutes or until clams open. Remove clams from shell and mince. Strain liquid remaining in pot. (Or: If using canned clams, drain and reserve liquor.) Cook salt pork until browned and crisp. Remove salt pork from pan, reserving 2 tablespoons drippings. In saucepan, add onion and cook until tender. Add clam liquor and potatoes. Bring to a boil and simmer until potatoes are tender. Pour milk over saltines and let stand until soft. Stir milk, half and half, reserved salt pork, and margarine into chowder mixture. Heat until hot enough to serve. Garnish with chopped parsley. Makes 6 servings.

MINESTRONE SOUP

3 pounds beef soup bones
4 quarts cold water
1 tablespoon salt
1/3 teaspoon pepper
1 bay leaf
1 clove garlic, minced
2 cups chopped cabbage
1 1/2 cups diced carrot
1 cup sliced celery
1 1-pound can tomatoes
1 1-pound can kidney beans, undrained
1 10-ounce package frozen peas
1 cup broken spaghetti

In large kettle combine soup bones and water. Bring to boil and skim if needed. Add salt, pepper, bay leaf and garlic. Cover and simmer 3 hours or until meat is tender. Remove meat from bones and return meat to soup along with vegetables. Cover and simmer 30 minutes or until vegetables are tender. Add spaghetti. Cover and simmer 10 minutes. Taste and adjust seasonings. Serve topped with grated Parmesan cheese. Makes 10 to 12 servings.

TWO-BEAN CHOWDER

1 cup dried small white navy beans
1 cup dried red beans
2 quarts water
1 cup minced onion
3/4 cup diced celery
3/4 cup diced carrot
1 clove garlic, minced
1/8 teaspoon pepper
1 1/2 cups milk, scalded
Salt and pepper

Soak beans in water overnight; do not drain. Then add ham hocks, cover and simmer 1 1/2 hours. Remove ham hocks, cut meat from bones and return meat to soup. Add onion, celery, carrot, garlic and pepper. Cover; simmer 1 hour. Add milk; cook until steaming hot; do not boil. Season to taste with salt and pepper. Makes 6 to 8 servings.

CREOLE SEAFOOD GUMBO

1/4 cup butter or margarine
2 tablespoons all-purpose flour
2 cups liquid (water and a little juice from seafood)
2 cups cut okra (fresh, frozen or canned)
2 cups peeled and cubed tomatoes (fresh or canned)
1 large onion, chopped
1 small green pepper, chopped
1 teaspoon Tabasco sauce
1/8 teaspoon thyme
1 bay leaf
2 cups shrimp, crab meat, oysters, or a combination (fresh, frozen or canned)
3 cups hot cooked rice

Melt butter in saucepan. Blend in flour and cook over low heat, stirring constantly, until dark brown. Add liquid, okra, tomatoes, onion, pepper, Tabasco sauce, thyme and bay leaf. Bring to a boil. Then cover and simmer for 30 to 40 minutes, stirring occasionally. Add seafood and cook 10-15 minutes longer. Remove bay leaf. Serve with mound of hot rice in center. Serves 6.

HEARTY VEAL SHANK AND VEGETABLE SOUP

4 pounds veal cross cut shanks, cut 1 1/2 inches thick
3 to 4 tablespoons olive oil
1 1/2 cups chopped onion
3 garlic cloves, minced
1 can (14 1/2 or 16 ounces) whole peeled tomatoes
2 1/2 cups water
3/4 cup dry white wine
2 teaspoons each dried basil and thyme leaves
1 teaspoon salt
1/2 teaspoon freshly ground black pepper
3 medium carrots, thinly sliced (about 1 cup)
1 can (16 to 19 ounces) cannellini (white kidney beans), well drained*
2 cups spinach strips, lightly packed (about 3 ounces spinach leaves

Brown veal shanks (1/2 at a time) in 2 to 3 tablespoons oil in Dutch oven or stock pot over medium heat. Remove shanks; reserve. Add 1 tablespoon oil to pan if needed. Cook onion and garlic until tender, about 5 minutes, stirring frequently and scraping up any browned bits. Stir in tomatoes with liquid, breaking up tomatoes with spoon. Add water, wine, basil, thyme, salt and pepper to pan. Return shanks to pan; bring to a boil. Reduce heat to low. Cover tightly and simmer 1 hour or until meat is tender. Remove shanks from pan; cool to touch. Remove meat from shanks and return to pan; discard bones. Add carrots; continue cooking, covered, until carrots are crisp-tender, about 5 minutes. Stir in beans and spinach; heat through. 6 servings.
*Or 16 ounce cans of great northern or navy beans, well drained, may be substituted.

BREAKFAST ON THE DREARY SIDE

All the way from Amarillo on to Dallas and right through the two-hour traffic jam that held us up just short of the junction of Interstate 635 with the east-west route of I-20, Tony and I pushed our heavily-loaded Dodge Caravan to the maximum in the drenching, angry, heavy early-December rain that never seemed to let up. Loaded with video cameras, film and hunting gear for a filming trip to hunt ducks in the flooded timberlands of southern Arkansas, we'd been on the road for almost two days now and we were struggling against the clock to meet our partner at the Monroe, Louisiana, airport, and then go on to the small town of Felsenthal in southern Arkansas where we'd rendezvous with our local hunters.

Finally, we broke out of the stalled traffic and headed east toward Louisiana but the rain never let up. And, at midnight when the three of us from Montana, cameramen Gary Holmes and Tony Schoonen and I, drove wearily to our meeting place at the locks-dam on the Ouachita River just outside Felsenthal, we didn't need any local experts to explain why the low-lying timberlands in the area flooded at this time of year. We'd seen more rain in our drive across Texas, northern Louisiana and the final leg of our journey into southern Arkansas than we'd experience in a couple of years in Montana.

Then, upon our rendezvous near midnight with local duck calling experts, brothers Mike and Roger Morton, from El Dorado, Arkansas, who would be our hosts and who also would serve as the featured hunters and callers in our videos, we boarded a pair of aluminum-hulled duck hunting boats crammed with our gear and headed for our "camp" — a floating cabin a couple of miles downriver, still in a pouring rain. A couple of hours later, our gear safely stowed inside the cabin, we slumped onto our cots and gratefully went to sleep, without supper, realizing there still had been no let-up in the rain.

We slept fitfully, as one might expect after traveling from Montana to this spot in Arkansas in two days and fighting a storm, plus sleeping on an uncomfortable cot, and knowing that, at best, we'd get only five or six hours of sleep.

But even that wasn't to be. Sometime soon, it seemed like only minutes, after we'd gotten into our bunks I heard the unmistakable sounds of someone working in the kitchen, getting a fire going in the wood cookstove, banging pans, washing something, and then the aroma of coffee filtered throughout the cabin. I groaned and, in the light that slanted into the room from the kitchen, looked at my watch. It was 3:30 a.m. and, reluctantly, I was about to experience a Southern hunting tradition: something totally alien and unexplainable to my Western, pragmatic notion that one should, when dead tired, get as much sleep as possible. These Southern boys, I was to learn, weren't about to let our weariness, the rain, or anything else, for that matter, stand in the way of tradition. You spend time, lots of time, around breakfast in a Southern hunting camp.

Now those of us from the West, being more pragmatic and less constrained by the notion of ancient customs, believe in having breakfast. But there's no ritual connected with it. We set aside just enough time to fix and consume our morning fare and then get on to the business at hand: going hunting. It's a routine that works. It's incredibly pragmatic. And we keep it simple, purposely, because it's functional and it gives us the most sleep, i.e., rest, that we can possibly get.

Civilization, it seems, has been around longer in the South. Their "breakfast" begins at 4 a.m. and eating is just part of it; getting the day going by talking with your friends, sharing what's on your mind regarding the hunt and the day, and who does what and goes where are all hashed and rehashed over cup upon never-empty cup of coffee.

That particular December morning, however, I resisted the tradition as long as I could. I was going to get every minute of sleep I could. But, with everybody else up and rattling around, it quickly became obvious that I wasn't going to get any more sleep. So, at the ungodly hour of 4:30 a.m., I was up for the day. I crawled into my pants and a shirt that still felt wet from the humidity and went into the kitchen. I edged a chair in between Tony and Gary and joined them and Mike at the table. Roger, over by the stove, grabbed a plate out of the pantry.

"Let me fix you up with some breakfast," he said in an accent that told me I was a long ways from home. I mumbled something about "seldom eating breakfast" and that "a cup of coffee or two will be enough for me" but Roger heaped the plate with a couple of eggs, a slice of ham, and thick, moist, steaming potatoes. "Better eat 'em," he said. "It'll be a long time until noon and we won't be eating anything before then. Besides, I put these smothered Cajun potatoes together especially for you guys."

So I did, we did, and what a treat. Roger's breakfast of ham and smothered Cajun potatoes was extraordinary, exquisite, supreme, awesome, one of the tastiest and most intriguing methods of preparing potatoes that I'd ever encountered. We each found ourselves, Gary and Tony and me, taking another helping and as we sat at the table over the next couple of hours we found ourselves coming to know something about our hosts, our new friends, who would share the coming days and the hunt with us. It was a breakfast like none other I'd ever had; indeed, it offered the first ray of sunshine we'd experience in the five days of dreary, rainy weather we experienced on a marvelous hunt and filming trip to Arkansas. Roger Morton had seen to that.

VEGETABLES

KIWI STYLE CAMP POTATOES

6-10 medium to large-sized potatoes
1 good-sized onion
Salt
Pepper
Vegetable oil, canola oil or shortening

Utensils needed:
10-inch cast iron skillet or equivalent
Skillet lid
Knife, fork or pancake turner

Peel potatoes. Slice lengthwise into halves, quarters, eighths and then 16ths in "kiwi" or New Zealand style to achieve a diagonally shaped unit that will not burn or scorch. Place in a deep 10-inch cast iron skillet or similar frying pan in which you've lightly covered the bottom with either vegetable oil, canola oil or shortening. Dice the onion and mix it uniformly with the potatoes. Add a few shakes of salt and pepper. Cover with lid over medium heat to achieve a combination of frying and steaming action. Check frequently and turn potatoes fairly often to prevent burning and achieve uniform cooking. When satisfied the potatoes are cooked, take off stove and let sit for a few minutes before serving. Excellent for serving plain or with gravy.

LEFTOVER FRIED POTATOES

Melt in a skillet 2 or more tablespoons fat. Add 2 cups cold, sliced, boiled potatoes. Salt and paprika. Optional: 1 or more teaspoons minced onion. Saute slowly until they are light brown.

ROGER MORTON'S SMOTHERED POTATOES

1 medium to large sized onion
5-6 medium sized potatoes
Italian salad dressing
Cajun seasoning
Salt and pepper

Cut onions up and put in good-sized skillet with three tablespoons of zesty Italian salad dressing. Leave skins on potatoes. Cut potatoes into small pieces and drop in skillet. Cover and simmer for about 30 minutes. Use salt and pepper as desired and cover with Tony Chacheres Cajun Seasoning.

Courtesy Roger Morton, El Dorado, Arkansas

HASHED BROWN POTATOES

Combine with a fork:
3 cups finely diced raw potatoes
1 teaspoon grated onion
1 tablespoon chopped parsley
1/2 teaspoon salt
1/4 teaspoon pepper
(1 teaspoon lemon juice)

Heat 3 tablespoons bacon drippings or oil in a 9 to 10 inch skillet. Spread the potato mixture over this. Press with a broad knife into a cake. Saute slowly, shaking from time to time to keep from sticking. When bottom is brown, cut in half and turn each half. Pour 1/4 cup cream over them. Brown the second side and serve hot.

BAKED BEANS

2 cans pork and beans (1 pound)
1 large onion, chopped
2 tablespoons fat or oil
1/4 cup catsup
1/4 cup brown sugar
1/2 teaspoon salt
1 tablespoon mustard

Mix together and pour into greased baking dish and bake at 325 degrees for 1 hour.

HARVARD BEETS

Wash 12 small beets, cook until soft. Remove skins, cut into small pieces or slices. You can also use canned or frozen beets.

Mix 1/2 cup sugar and 1/2 tablespoon cornstarch. Add 1/2 cup vinegar and boil 5 minutes. Pour over beets and let stand at low heat for 1/2 hour. Just before serving, add 2 tablespoons butter.

SHREDDED CARROTS

5 or 6 carrots
Salt
2 tablespoons butter

Coarsely shred 5 or 6 carrots. Season with 3/4 teaspoon salt. Cover, cook in 2 tablespoons butter 5 to 7 minutes.

CARROTS

1 cup sugar
1/4 teaspoon salt
1 tablespoon flour
2 tablespoons cornstarch
1 1/4 cup orange juice
1/4 cup lemon juice
1/2 cup water
1 tablespoon butter
Cooked carrots

Boil first 8 ingredients 3 minutes over low heat, remove and add grated rind of 3 oranges. Pour over cooked carrots. (Can also use sweet potatoes.)

GRILLED POTATOES

1/2 cup salad dressing
3 garlic cloves, minced
1/2 teaspoon paprika
1/4 teaspoon each of salt, pepper
3 baking potatoes, cut into 1/4 inch slices
1 large onion, sliced

Mix salad dressing and seasonings in large bowl until well blended. Stir in potatoes and onions to coat. Divide potato mixture evenly among six 12-inch square pieces of heavy-duty foil. Seal each to form packet. Place foil packets on grill over medium-hot coals (coals will have slight glow). Grill, covered, 25 to 30 minutes or until potatoes are tender. Six servings.

BEETS

1/2 cup chopped onions
1/4 cup chopped green peppers or parsley
4 cups diced, cooked beets
1/4 teaspoon salt

Simmer onions and peppers in a small amount of water. Add beets, simmer. Season to taste.

QUICK AND EASY SPAGHETTI SAUCE

1 13-ounce can of white hominy (drained)
1 15 1/2-ounce can of chili beans
1/2 cup diced onion
1 cup sour cream
1 4-ounce can chopped green chilies
1/2 teaspoon salt

Combine hominy, beans, onions and green chilies. Heat through then add sour cream. Heat until hot, serve over spaghetti noodles cooked according to directions on package. Can also use fettucini noodles or serve with corn bread. If you like it spicier, add chili powder to taste.

Courtesy Jane Karr, Stevensville, Montana

TOFU ENCHILADAS

1 package firm tofu
1 16-ounce can Mexican black or pinto beans
1/2 cup chopped onion
1/2 cup chopped celery
1/2 cup chopped broccoli
1/2 cup sliced olives
1/2 cup grated cheese
1 medium can enchilada sauce
10 - 12 corn shells
3 tablespoons oil

Rinse and pat dry tofu. In large skillet saute onions and diced or crumbled tofu in oil until light brown. Add celery and broccoli and cook 1 minute. Add 1/2 can enchilada sauce and drained beans. Layer bean mixture with olives and half of the cheese in corn shell. Roll and place seam side down in shallow baking dish. Cover enchiladas with remaining sauce and grated cheese. Bake 350 degrees for 30 minutes.

Note: You can substitute any vegetables you want. A great way to use leftovers.

Courtesy Karan Kunz, Boulder, Montana

GREEN BEANS

4 slices bacon
1/4 cup chopped onion
1 to 2 tablespoons tarragon vinegar
2 cups hot, drained green beans

Fry bacon till crisp, drain. Cook onion in 2 tablespoons bacon drippings till tender. Add vinegar. Season with salt and pepper. Pour over hot beans.

TEXTURED VEGETABLE PROTEIN & SPINACH LASAGNA

1 cup TVP soaked in 1 1/4 cup of boiling water; let set at least 5 minutes (For added flavor use powered veggie broth in soaking water).

1 chopped onion
2 cloves garlic
Saute in 2 tablespoons cooking oil. Stir in TVP. Set on low heat for 2-5 minutes.

Tomato Sauce:
32 ounces tomato sauce
6 ounces tomato paste
2 cups of water
2 tablespoons each: basil, oregano, brown sugar

Combine with TVP mixture and simmer while you make spinach filling.

10 ounces cooked spinach, chopped and drained (frozen can be used)
2 cups fat free cottage cheese
1/2 cup Parmesan cheese
2 eggs or 1 whole egg and 2 egg whites
1 pound grated mozzarella cheese (low fat)

Rinse in cold water 8 ounces of lasagna noodles (approximately 10-12 noodles)
Layer the ingredients into a 9x13 inch casserole:
1/4 sauce, 1/2 noodles
1/4 sauce, 1/2 mozzarella
ALL the spinach and remaining noodles
1/4 sauce and remaining mozzarella

Bake 60 minutes covered, then uncover and bake 10 minutes at 375 degrees. Remove from oven and let stand 10 minutes. This makes a nice large lasagna.

(Note: TVP is textured vegetable protein available at most health food stores.)

Courtesy Jane Karr, Stevensville, Montana

BULGUR STOVE-TOP CASSEROLE

1 cup bulgur
3 cups hot water
2 tablespoons oil
1/2 cup chopped green pepper
1/2 cup chopped zucchini
1 cup chopped green onions
1 cup peas (fresh or frozen)
1 1/2 cups V8 juice. If you like flavor use V8 that has added spices.
2 teaspoons lemon juice
1 teaspoon dried basil
1 teaspoon onion powder
1/2 teaspoon garlic powder
Salt to taste

Cook bulgur in 3 cups hot water over medium heat until dry and set aside. Saute in oil the pepper, onion, and zucchini until tender-crisp. Stir in juice, lemon, spices and bulgur. Heat to a boil. Cover and let simmer 15 minutes or until liquid is absorbed. Stir in green peas. If fresh peas are used, blanch first. If frozen peas are used, run hot tap water over them for a couple of seconds and then add to mixture. Stir and serve. Makes 6 to 8 servings.

Courtesy Jane Karr, Stevensville, Montana

NATURE'S BURGERS

1 block firm tofu-drained and mashed
1 whole egg
2 egg whites
2 teaspoons baking powder
1 teaspoon salt
1/2 teaspoon garlic powder
2-3 tablespoons wheat germ
1/2 to 1 cup grated carrot
3 tablespoons dry parsley
1 cup minced green onion (can substitute dry onion)

If mixture is to moist add approximately 1/2 cup dry oats. Let set for 15 minutes. Form into patties or drop by large spoonsfull in hot shallow oil. Fry until golden brown on both sides. Cook at least 5 minutes on each side using medium to low heat. Cover while frying.

Serve as main dish or use on buns with your favorite fixings. Makes 8 burgers.

Courtesy Jane Karr, Stevensville, Montana

BARBECUED POTATOES

Potatoes
Onions
Salt
Pepper

Slice potatoes and onions. Butter the middle of a square piece of aluminum foil. Layer potato and onion on foil, sprinkle with salt and pepper. Fold up and put on the side of the coals, turning often. Cook 45 minutes being careful not to burn.

SOUTH OF THE BORDER FRIED RICE

3-4 cups cooked rice (brown or white)
1 cup corn (canned or frozen)
1-2 cups cooked dark red kidney beans
2-3 fresh tomatoes, cubed (or 1 15-ounce can chopped tomatoes, drained)
1 bunch green onions diced
2 tablespoons oil (can omit oil and use water if you want to cook oil free)
1 tablespoon chili powder
1/2 teaspoon garlic powder
Salt to taste

Saute rice, corn, beans and onions until hot over medium heat. Add spices and tomatoes. Cook on low heat until tomatoes are hot. Serves 4 to 6.

Courtesy Jane Karr, Stevensville, Montana

EASY BAKE BURRITOS

1 16-ounce can of fat free refried beans or 2 cups of cooked mashed pinto beans
1 bunch chopped green onions (dry onions can be substituted)
1 4-ounce can of chopped olives
1 4-ounce can of chopped green chilies
1 cup grated cheddar cheese

Mix all ingredients together. Warm tortilla so it will roll easy. Put 1/3 cup of mixture on tort, fold over ends. Put fold side down on cookie sheet. When all mixture is used spray or brush with cooking oil. Bake approximately 20 minutes at 350 degrees. Do Not Brown. Eat them hot or cold. Great for taking camping or fishing. Serve with salsa or sour cream if you desire but they are very tasty plain. Makes approximately 10 burritos.

Courtesy Jane Karr, Stevensville, Montana

INDEX

CASSEROLES AND MAIN DISHES

CASSEROLES AND MAIN DISHES (Continued)

DESSERTS

DESSERTS (Continued)

MEATS

MEATS (Continued)

WILD GAME AND BISON

WILD GAME AND BISON (Continued)

SALADS

SANDWICHES

SNACKS

SOUPS

SOUPS (Continued)

VEGETABLES

LISTING OF BOOKS

Additional copies of **CAMP COOKBOOK**, and many other of Stoneydale Press' books on outdoor recreation, big game hunting, or historical reminisces centered around the Northern Rocky Mountain region, are available at many book stores and sporting goods stores, or direct from Stoneydale Press. If you'd like more information, or like to make an order, you can contact us by calling a toll free number, **1-800-735-7006,** or writing the address at the bottom of the page. Here's a partial listing of some of the books that are available:

Cookbooks

Camp Cookbook, Featuring Recipes for Fixing Both at Home and in Camp, With Field Stories by Dale A. Burk, 216 pages

Cooking for Your Hunter, By Miriam Jones, 180 pages

Historical Reminisces, Hunting Books

Indian Trails & Grizzly Tales, By Bud Cheff Sr., 212 pages, available in clothbound and softcover editions

They Left Their Tracks, By Howard Copenhaver, Recollections of Sixty Years as a Wilderness Outfitter, 192 pages, clothbound or softcover editions (One of our all-time most popular books.)

More Tracks, By Howard Copenhaver, 78 Years of Mountains, People & Happiness, 180 pages, clothbound or softcover editions

Mules & Mountains, By Margie E. Hahn, the story of Walt Hahn, Forest Service Packer, 164 pages, clothbound or softcover editions

Montana Hunting Guide, By Dale A. Burk, the most comprehensive and fact-filled guidebook available on hunting in Montana, 192 pages, clothbound or softcover editions

Bugling for Elk, By Dwight Schuh, the bible on hunting early-season elk. A recognized classic, 164 pages, softcover edition only

Western Hunting Guide, By Mike Lapinski, the most thorough guide on hunting the western states available. A listing of where-to-go in the western states alone makes the book a valuable reference tool, 168 pages, clothbound or softcover editions

STONEYDALE PRESS PUBLISHING COMPANY

205 Main Street • Drawer B
Stevensville, Montana 59870
Phone: 406-777-2729